Anna's
Courage

ISBN: 978-1-63813-354-4

Cover and interior design: Kristi Yoder

Cover and interior artwork: Laura Yoder

Printed in the USA

Published by:

CAM Books
P.O. Box 355
Berlin, Ohio 44610 USA
Phone: 330.893.4828
Fax: 330.893.4893
cambooks.org

Anna's Courage

Wait on the Lord:
be of good courage, and he
shall strengthen thine heart:
wait, I say, on the Lord.
Psalm 27:14

Lily A. Bear

Table of Contents

Prologue

I believe I felt my first real need for courage on that June day in 1929 when I overheard my father, Bernhard Williams, say to my mother, "Marie, I've been trying to farm ever since we were married. But instead of getting easier, it seems to be getting harder. Either the landlord sells the farm we are renting, or the crops do not make the farm payments—and we need to move. Something needs to change."

It made me sad to hear Papa's words, but at eleven years of age, I was old enough to understand why our family had not always lived at the same farm. We had been living in our present house—less than two miles from Kingman,

Alberta—only since March. Before that, we had lived for eight months in a shed-house on another farm, a situation not nearly as nice as our current one.

A few weeks later we were at Grandpa King's place one Sunday, and I heard the men talking again. "This weather is not good!" Uncle David said. "These dry summers are bringing more and more dust storms and are harming our crops." I could hear the worry in the men's voices as they talked about low grain prices. My stomach tightened with fear.

We didn't visit my grandparents or Uncle David and his family very often because they lived near Tofield, about an hour from our home. I had been so happy traveling toward church near Tofield that morning. The weather had been perfect for the long drive with our horse and buggy. After church we had eaten dinner with Grandma and Grandpa King in their cute little house beside Uncle David's big farmhouse. But after hearing the discussion in the house...well, my afternoon was largely spoiled. As I played with my cousins, I tried to forget the worry in the men's voices—but I couldn't shake it off.

My brother Charles and I were enjoying the summer break from school. Charles was ten years old, a year younger than I, and we were both old enough to help with the work. Summer days at our home were filled with lots of work, but Mama had a way of making the work fun.

As we drove home later that afternoon, I was thinking, *Hooray! Hooray for summer!*

But that summer turned out quite different than I expected.

It was the summer I learned the meaning of the word *courage.*

Map of the
KINGMAN, ALBERTA, CANADA area

ST ALBERT

EDMONTON

Beaver hill
Lake

TOFIELD

Uncle David +
Grandpa King's
place

Church

KINGMAN

Shirley's
place

Gopher town

Anna's
place

crow's
nest

Pigeon
Lake

CAMROSE

1

Strawberry Surprise

"Goodbye, Anna!" Shirley called as we parted ways at the end of the school lane. "See you tomorrow!" I headed east into the countryside while Shirley turned west down Main Street of our little town of Kingman, Alberta.

I looked back at the town buildings gleaming white in the sunshine. The church stood across the road from our one-room school. Next to it was a garage, a general store (or the "Mercantile," as Shirley called it), the bank, and the town hall and post office both in the same building. Near the end of the street, a red grain elevator towered above the town with "Alberta Wheat Pool" painted on its sides in big white letters.

We could see the elevator from quite a distance. My ten-year-old brother Charles told me it had to be big because it held forty thousand bushels of wheat! I shook my head. That was simply too much wheat to comprehend.

Anna's Courage

As I began the walk home, I smiled as an idea popped into my mind. Turning around, I cupped my hands around my mouth and hollered at Shirley's retreating back, "Shirley! Have fun milking the goats!" I started to laugh as I waited for her reply.

"Please!" Shirley whirled around. She stomped her foot and pinched her nose. "I would—I would—rather—eat strawberries!" she yelled.

It was always fun to see Shirley's reaction when I mentioned the goats. "I don't know why my father insists on keeping those goats!" she had moaned many times. "He just says I need the responsibility. I hate being the only child!" And Shirley would stomp her foot just as she had now.

I couldn't imagine stomping my foot, but then Shirley did other things I would never have thought of doing. Yet I liked her. She never laughed at my homemade clothes or my plain lunches of brown buttered bread.

To think I once dreaded being her seatmate! My thoughts flew back several months to the first day Charles and I had attended this new school in Kingman. Since Shirley's papa owned the Mercantile, she lived close to school in a big white house with yellow trim around the windows and front door. The house was nicely painted and had a wide porch running along the entire front—while my family lived in an old weather-beaten farmhouse. I wondered if our house had ever been painted and what color it might have been.

I had been afraid of Shirley. Would the girl wearing store-bought dresses and stylish shoes make fun of me? But the welcoming smile she gave me when I slid into the seat beside her on my first day of school had changed my mind. Shirley never made fun of others and was quick to share her things. Everyone in school liked her. It didn't take long for the two of us to develop a special friendship. We were both eleven years old.

Our friendship had been cemented the day the rest of my family drove into the schoolyard just as school was being dismissed, taking Charles and me by surprise. Five-year-old Dora and three-year-old Paul, our younger siblings, were all eyes as the students crowded around the buggy.

"You're so lucky, Anna!" Shirley had declared fiercely. "I wish I had brothers and sisters like you do!"

Shirley had reached for Baby Mary. "May I please hold her, Mrs. Williams?" she had asked. Mary went to her without a fuss, and I was surprised at the joy on Shirley's face.

"An-na! An-na Ma-rie Will-iams!" Hearing my name jerked me back to the present. I shaded my eyes against the sun as Shirley shouted, "Do you think they ripened over the weekend?"

"What?" I yelled back.

"The strawberries!" Shirley replied.

Strawberries? Oh! Strawberries! I set out at a run toward my friend. "Do you know where there are some?" I panted when I reached her. "Oh, Shirley, do you think they're ready? Let's go find out!" With childish abandon, she grabbed my hand as we dashed down the dusty road.

In minutes, we reached an empty lot. "Here we are!" Shirley puffed. "This is the best place to find wild strawberries."

"Won't our mamas be surprised!" I gasped as I flopped down onto the scraggly grass. Shirley didn't answer. She was too busy scouring the area for the tiny, sweet, hidden berries.

Shirley popped a ripe berry into her mouth. "Mmm! They taste marvelous! I think we're the first ones to find them!"

I gently lifted the leaves of the low plants beside me, savoring the sight of ripened fruit. *Mama is going to be so happy!* I thought. I relished the sweetness of a berry as it melted in my mouth. Shirley was blissfully eating every one she picked, but I allowed myself only one.

Opening my tin lunch pail, I gently laid a handful of berries on the bottom. *Maybe Mama will let me make a cream cake for supper! Yum! Strawberries and warm cream cake!*

"I'll help you." Shirley's voice startled me as she plopped her handful of berries into my lard pail.

"Th-thanks!" I sputtered in surprise. "But don't you want to keep yours?"

"No." Shirley shook her head. "I'll eat what I want here.

My mother wouldn't like to be bothered with these little berries. She gets her strawberries from Mrs. Madison's garden patch. I heard her say they should be ready in a week or so. That reminded me of these berries, but I forgot all about them until you mentioned the goats."

"Then it's a good thing I did!" We laughed together as heat shimmered across the countryside. We quickly picked every red berry we could find.

It was unusually hot for the third week of June. Tomorrow would be the last day of school. At noon, the annual picnic would begin. I would probably not see Shirley all summer, so I enjoyed every minute of this time together.

"I can't thank you enough!" I said, looking around for the last berries. I gave Shirley a huge smile as I carefully put the lid on my lunch pail. "My family, especially Mary, is

Anna's Courage

going to love these! I'll be sure to mention that you helped pick them!"

"You had better! Or I might steal Mary away from you tomorrow!"

"I'll tell them," I promised as we once more parted ways. Dust swirled around me as I hurried up the road. Charles had stayed at home to help Papa with first-cutting hay, and I hoped Mama was not worrying about my being late.

"Mama! I'm home!" I called, pushing open the screen door. No one answered. The house was quiet.

Where is everybody? Maybe Mama took drinking water out to Papa and Charles. I dipped myself a cup of water from the bucket in the corner of the cupboard. *It's definitely hot enough for a drink!*

"Guess I might as well clean these berries." My words sounded loud in the empty kitchen, and I hurried upstairs to change out of my school dress. Hanging it on a nail and slipping into my everyday dress, I hurried to finish my surprise before the rest of the family arrived home.

I was placing the bowl of washed, stemmed strawberries on the table when I heard the horse and buggy drive in. In a flash, I was out the back door and running down the footpath to meet Mama and the younger ones.

"There is a surprise on the table!" I sang out before anyone could ask what I had been doing while they were gone.

Smiling at Mama, I held the horse as she climbed out of the buggy.

"I picked strawberries for supper," I said. "I even had time to wash them!"

Mama's eyes lit up in surprise. "Strawberries! That will be wonderful! I'll have you stir up a cream cake to go with them."

I nodded happily as I unhitched old Ned and led him to the barn. *To think Shirley's mama does not like wild berries!* I shook my head in disbelief.

I did not see the weather-beaten house, the leaning buggy shed attached to the barn, or the patches of high weeds along the fencerow. Instead, I saw the shining faces of my siblings and thought of the fun and laughter we shared as we played hide-and-seek in the evenings.

I pictured Papa, black with dust, coming in from the field, his eyes crinkling in laughter as he swung Mary high into the air. I thought of Mama singing a familiar hymn as she pulled hot loaves of golden bread from the wood-burning cookstove.

Anna's Courage

"I would never trade places with Shirley," I said to old Ned as I led him to the barnyard. "I'd rather have this!" My arm swept out in an arc, smacking Ned on his side. The horse didn't flinch. He just kept walking toward the water trough. He gulped down water and then plodded into his stall. I laughed and ran into the house.

"What a treat!" Papa beamed later that evening as he dug into his bowl of cake, berries, and milk.

Mary banged her spoon on the table. *More!* she seemed to say as Mama fed her another bite.

"Shirley helped me pick the berries," I informed my family. "I would never have been able to pick this many in the short time I had."

Bang! Bang! went Mary's spoon, and everyone laughed as she blew bubbles through the crumbs sticking to her round little mouth.

"I will thank Shirley tomorrow," Mama said as she reached for a cloth to wipe up the mess Mary had made.

"She said she would steal Mary for the day if I didn't tell you she helped."

Dora's eyes widened in alarm. "No!" she wailed. "I want to keep Mary!"

"Hush, Dora. That's not what she meant." I put my arm around her. "She just wants to hold Mary and play with her on the day of the picnic. She didn't mean she would keep her. Remember how there are no other children at Shirley's house? She has no one to play with—no little sister or brother to hold."

"Just the goats," Charles said, and we burst out laughing.

The sun disappeared behind the evergreen trees, and the evening shadows gathered as Mama stacked the dirty supper dishes and Papa and Charles left the kitchen.

I took down the chipped enamel dishpan hanging by the pantry and set it on the edge of the stove. Lifting the reservoir lid of the stove, I scooped out several dippers of hot water. I carried the dishpan to the table and tested the temperature with my hand. *Just right,* I decided. Picking up a chunk of homemade lye soap, I rubbed it vigorously over the dishrag until milky curdles appeared in the water. Back and forth, back and forth, I rubbed the soap over the rag until the water was sudsy and silky smooth and would not leave soap scum on the dishes.

"Can we play 'Family'?" Dora asked as she picked up the drying towel.

"That sounds like fun!" I agreed. "What people do you want our soup bowls to be?"

"Um…" Dora's mouth puckered as she stared at the bowls. "Maybe Grandma and Grandpa and the cousins?"

"That sounds good! Grandpa and Grandma came over for supper tonight because…" I began. I then stopped the story and let Dora pick it up. It was fun to pretend the dishes were members of a family. We took turns making up a story about what the dish family might be doing.

"Today is Papa's birthday," Dora continued. "Mama wanted to surprise Papa with the first strawberries, so she had Grandpa and Grandma come. They were happy to come because…"

"Grandma can't pick strawberries anymore!" I added. We both giggled at the thought of Grandma picking strawberries while holding her cane. Dora paused to think what should happen next as she wiped another clean bowl. One rule in playing the game was you had to keep working as you made up the story.

"Anna," Dora begged, "tell me again how you started playing this game."

"Well, when I was about your age, I hated doing dishes!" I wrinkled my nose, making her giggle. "Every day I had to do the dishes, and I didn't always do them cheerfully. One day I was complaining, so Mama said, 'Anna, if you don't work, then you can't eat.'

"I didn't believe Mama would really let me go hungry, so the next time I washed the dishes I was whining again.

"Mama was tired of it. 'Anna,' she said, 'today you can choose what you want to do. You can either wash the dishes cheerfully and then enjoy a snack, or you can go play and

I will do the dishes. But before you decide, I want you to remember the Bible verse we talked about. Do you remember it?'

"I nodded. I did remember it: 'If any man would not work, neither should he eat.' I knew the verse, but I still didn't think Mama would refuse to give me something to eat if I was hungry. 'If you choose not to wash the dishes, you can't have anything to eat until suppertime,' Mama warned.

"We had just eaten dinner and I wasn't one bit hungry, so I decided to go play. I was so happy when I ran outdoors! For once I didn't have to wash those horrid dishes!

"I played for a long, long time. When I thought it was almost suppertime, I went into the house. Mama had baked bread, and six big loaves were cooling on the table. Suddenly I was very hungry. 'Mama, is it almost suppertime?' I asked. 'I'm hungry!'

" 'No, it's not even three o'clock yet,' Mama replied.

"I was shocked! It was still a long time until supper! I was tired of playing and was hungry for a piece of Mama's good, crusty bread. But I was also worried. Would Mama make me wait until supper? If only I had helped with the dishes, then I could eat a piece of bread!

"I saw a stack of dirty baking dishes on the counter, but I didn't see any dirty dinner dishes. Mama looked hot and tired, and I felt bad for not helping her. I started to cry and told her I was sorry. I said I would help her the rest of the afternoon. And I did. But I had to wait to taste Mama's delicious bread until suppertime.

"That's when I started pretending the dirty dishes were people. Every time I washed dishes, I made up a story. Sometimes the forks and spoons were little children at the hospital. I pretended the hospital needed extra helpers, so Mama had sent me to help. Pretending helped make washing dishes a fun job!"

Dora smiled up at me. "I'm glad you started playing the game. How old was I when you started playing it?"

"You were about Mary's age," I replied. "I was six and had started school. You weren't old enough to help me. It was just me and my imagination!"

We shared a smile, and Dora continued with the game. "All us cousins decided to do the huge stack of dishes so Mama and Grandma could visit." Dora picked up a spoon. "This is Irene," she said. "Irene started crying because…"

Mama smiled at our chatter and the dish game. She picked up little Mary, who was clinging to her dress. "Are you girls finished? It's time to get ready for bed. Tomorrow will be here before we know it."

2

School Adventures

"Anna, stop! Listen!" Charles gave my arm a tug, and I stopped walking. "What do you think is happening at school?" I could hear distant shouts and peals of laughter coming from the schoolyard.

"It sounds like fun," Charles said. "I'm going to see what they're doing." He took off running while I followed close behind. As we neared the schoolhouse, we spied our friends along the creek at the edge of the schoolyard. Several of the boys had long poles. As I watched, Harley ran toward the creek bank. Thrusting his pole into the ground, he sprang up and swung in a high arc to the other side of the creek.

Then Joe gave a whoop as he sailed across.

Splash! The girls lining the bank screamed when Percy missed the opposite bank and tumbled into the water. Quick as a flash he scrambled out, dripping wet. "It's just water!" he yelled to the girls as he picked up his pole and stepped back for another try.

"Watch!" he yelled, running toward the creek.

"Yeah, yeah, for Percy! Yeah, yeah, for Percy!" The chant swelled as the girls got caught up in the excitement. Younger

Anna's Courage

students were clapping their hands and jumping up and down. I picked up my skirt and ran toward the action.

"Come! Hurry! This is so much fun!" Shirley called to me, pulling me closer to the bank. "Harley and George were practicing this at home. They brought a bunch of poles along to school today! Teacher says we can take rides if we're careful. Won't this be a fun last day? I can't wait to take another ride!" She threw a mischievous glance my way.

I didn't share her enthusiasm. It looked like fun, but it also looked scary. It wasn't too bad for a boy to fall into the water. But a girl? I decided then and there I would only watch. Shirley could take a turn if she wanted to, but not me. Besides, I didn't think Mama and Papa would approve.

I held my breath as Charles grabbed a pole and heaved himself into the air. I relaxed when he landed safely, flashing a grin at me. "It might be easier than it looks," I admitted to Shirley. "If it were only us girls, I would try it."

Just then Miss Peterson stepped outside and rang the bell. The poles were reluctantly dropped, but no one complained; noon would soon be here. The students from all eight grades formed an orderly line as we filed into the classroom and stood beside our desks.

"Good morning, boys and girls," Miss Peterson greeted us.

"Good morning, Miss Peterson!" we answered in unison.

"Let's begin our last day of school with the Lord's Prayer."

Nineteen heads bowed, and nineteen pairs of eyes closed. The eighteen students followed their teacher's example of reverence and began reciting the familiar Lord's Prayer. "Our Father which art in heaven…"

"You may be seated. We will now take our final roll call." Miss Peterson smiled and opened her book.

I stiffened as Harley, who sat in front of Shirley and me, looked back at us and snickered. I gritted my teeth as he kicked back with his foot, jarring our desk and sending his pencil clattering to the floor. He stooped down to retrieve it and then whacked my toe when he picked it up. I caught his wink as Shirley stuck out her tongue at him.

Harley, the class bully, was the blot on an otherwise happy school term. How I dreaded correcting his papers when we had to pass our work to the person behind us. He was always turning around, making horrid faces, and letting Shirley or me know he expected us to mark every answer correct! *As though I would cheat,* I seethed.

Mama said Harley did irritating things to get attention. "If you don't get irked at his actions and treat him respectfully, he might stop," she had said.

Maybe Mama is right! I thought guiltily. *But he is so hard to like! He's always showing off or being mean!*

Miss Peterson kept a well-ordered school—using the strap on anyone who misbehaved. She was firm but fair. Harley was the only student who wasn't fazed by her discipline. Or at least he acted as if he didn't care. I sighed. *Maybe I should try Mama's suggestion. It surely wouldn't hurt for this last day of school.*

A smile tugged at the corners of my mouth. *I'll suggest it to Shirley at recess! And until then, I'll give Harley a smile every time he turns around or does something annoying. Shirley will think I've lost my mind. But maybe she'll catch on and try it too.*

The desk jolted as Harley half turned and gave us a nasty scowl. His dark eyebrows drawn together, he quickly whispered, "Just you wait!" before Miss Peterson turned away from the blackboard. I sent a quick smile at him before focusing my attention on the teacher. Shirley raised her eyebrows at me as Harley sat up in his seat. Twice more Harley scowled—and twice more I returned a smile. Shirley watched me, giving a slight nod as if she understood.

Good! I think Shirley knows what I'm doing. Maybe she'll try it too! I hoped my smile would tell her what I wanted to say.

"It's time for the spelling bee!" Miss Peterson announced. She lined us up on opposite sides of the room.

Harley's turn to spell came just before mine, and he missed the word *apostrophe.* I watched as he sullenly took his seat.

"Apostrophe," Miss Peterson called, looking at me. My mind suddenly went blank. Try as I might, I could not remember how to spell it. "A-p-p-o-s-t-r-o-p-h-y," I spelled haltingly. I knew it was wrong but was helpless to correct it.

"Wrong. Verna, apostrophe." Frowning, I returned to my seat.

"A-p-o-s-t-r-o-p-h-e." As my friend Verna spelled it correctly, I realized Harley had only missed the *e* at the end.

"You almost had it," I whispered to him as I sat down. "I wasn't even close!" Surprise flashed across his face, and he gave a slight nod. I noticed he did not try to trip the other students when they passed his desk, as he often did.

The morning continued with a blur of activity. Desks needed to be cleaned out and artwork taken down from the walls. Just before dismissal, Miss Peterson rang the bell. "Please return to your seats," she called.

We slid into our seats and waited expectantly for her to dismiss us. Once the room was quiet, she said, "I want to thank all of you who did your best this year. If you think you failed in this, most of you will be returning next year and will have a chance to improve.

"Best wishes to you, Ruby, as you graduate with excellent grades. I know you will be an asset in whatever work you are engaged in, even if it is simply being employed at home. Homemaking is an important role to fill.

"Joe, you too receive my highest regards as you fill your place alongside your father on the farm. Farming is a wonderful occupation with many diverse talents needed to operate efficiently.

"To the rest of you, I hope you have a good summer. Make the most of each day. Do your best in whatever you are doing. It takes hard, diligent work to complete your tasks correctly. Most of you have had good practice this school year in hard, diligent work. Carry that work ethic home with you, and you will never be sorry. I have enjoyed being your teacher. Goodbye, students. Class dismissed."

As soon as the boys were outside, whoops filled the air and I heard Harley shouting, "No more studies, no more books, no more Teacher's dirty looks."

"He's disgusting." Verna voiced the older girls' sentiments. "If anyone deserves a dirty look, it's him. He certainly tries to earn them!"

"I know I will miss school," Shirley was quick to say. "I love coming, and I'm going to miss all my friends." She looped her arm through mine as we headed for our teacher's desk. "Thank you for being our teacher, Miss Peterson."

A wagon clattered into the schoolyard. Parents were arriving for the picnic! The schoolroom emptied as we hurried outside, not wanting to miss any of the action. Several men were unloading sawhorses and long planks from their wagons. They soon had makeshift tables set up in the shade along the school's north side.

"Did your mama bring her delicious cinnamon rolls?"

Shirley asked, eyeing the two tables loaded with food.

"Over there," I pointed, pleased that she wanted one. On the rare occasion she brought a cinnamon roll to school, Shirley always traded her store-bought treat for my home-made one.

"Yum!" she said. "My mouth is already watering! Your mama makes the best rolls I ever tasted!"

When it was finally time to eat, Shirley and I filled our tin plates from pots of baked beans swimming with rich, fatty pork, dishes of hot potatoes, and crocks of potato salad. "Mama brought these," I said as I dished out a spoonful of thick, creamy noodles.

"Did you help her make them?" When I nodded yes, Shirley murmured, "Lucky you. It would be so much fun to do everything you do!"

Fun? I had never thought of work as fun. *Would Shirley think it was fun to turn the handle on the butter churn until her arm ached? Or haul in bucket after bucket of well water to keep the stove reservoir filled?* And every week I needed to wash and dry the lamps. What a tiresome job! First I had to crumple a sheet of paper from an old Eaton's catalog, then insert the paper inside each sooty glass chimney to wipe off the worst of the soot. Once that was done, I had to wash each chimney with soapy water, rinse it in more water, then dry and polish the glass until it shone. No streaks were allowed, or I had to polish it again! One lamp wouldn't have been so bad, but we had three lamps to clean!

Chores greeted us each morning—barn chores, kitchen chores, baking and laundry chores, garden chores. The list seemed endless. *And Shirley thinks our work is fun?*

"Don't you want any custard or cake?" Shirley gave me a poke in the back. Looking down, I realized we had almost passed the desserts while I was daydreaming. "I got the biggest cinnamon roll in the pan," she said. She gave a sigh of delight as we went to sit with the other schoolgirls along the creek bank.

It was late in the afternoon when our tired family climbed into the buggy and headed home. "I had so much fun!" Dora yawned as she nestled against me.

"Yes, it was a good day!" I agreed. I settled back against the side of the wagon to recall the pleasant picnic. There had been stiff competition between the ball teams, and the game ended with our team losing by only one run.

The little girls had been delighted when Verna suggested we big girls could turn the long skipping rope so that two or three little girls could jump together. I smiled as I remembered their happy chanting. "Grace, Grace, powdered her face. How many boxes did she use? One, two, three, four…" The counting would go on until someone stopped the rope with her feet.

The pole-jumping across the creek had brought both fathers and mothers over to watch. Shirley was the only girl who tried it, and wild cheering erupted from us girls each time she vaulted the water. *Maybe it will work out for me to visit her this summer. She could show me how to pole jump.* She had said she practiced after school for several days that week.

"I don't remember how many times I missed the bank or fell down until I learned the right thrust," she said. "Mama wasn't happy with my wet, muddy dress, but she didn't forbid me from jumping! I was afraid she would. I showed Papa what I could do, and I think he was rather proud of me!" She giggled.

I smiled to myself as I recalled the graceful way Shirley had glided across the creek. Not the way the boys swung, wild and high, but with one swift push of her pole she had skimmed the top of the water before landing lightly on the opposite bank. *I will miss Shirley—but maybe I'll ask Mama if she can come and spend a day with me. I'll tell her that Shirley wants to do all my FUN WORK!*

We were putting our picnic things away when Dora came racing into the house. "The peddler is here!" she panted. "He's coming in the lane!"

3

The Peddler

The peddler! I stopped washing the picnic dishes, dropped the dishrag into the wash pan, and hurried outside. I loved seeing all the things the peddler carried with him. Maybe, just maybe, this would be the year we could afford to buy real dress fabric. I smiled to myself.

I looked down at my dress made from used flour sacks. I did not mind wearing flour-sack fabric at home or school, but I wished I could have a Sunday dress made of real fabric. Edith had one. It was hard not to be envious of her soft fabric with its dainty floral pattern. A little sigh escaped my mouth as I neared the parked wagon cart. *I better not even think of it. Then I won't be disappointed.*

I knew Mama hoped we could sell some extra garden produce for some spending money. She had mentioned it to Papa when we planted the garden and had listed a few needs. "Charles's boots will be too small by next winter, and Anna has outgrown hers too. But maybe the garden will not do well. If it doesn't, we will still have plenty of laughter!" With a soft chuckle, she had repeated one of her sayings: "Money is scarce but laughter is plenty. I am richly blessed to have a family that laughs together." I thought of this as the peddler lifted the sidewall on his cart to display his goods.

It always fascinated me to watch him pull down the brace board fastened to the sidewall. This board held up the sidewall when he placed it in a special little groove and fastened it with a hook. After propping up the wall, he folded out a wide shelf from inside the cart and secured it in much the same way.

When he had his cart opened up, it made a perfect traveling store. The raised sidewall provided a roof and revealed his wares hanging inside. The shelf provided a place to set baskets filled with smaller items such as combs, spools of thread, pencils, and buttons.

Bolts of pretty fabric stood at one side of the opening. Colors and floral patterns bloomed before my eyes. Oh, how

The Peddler

I wanted that blue piece with sprays of tiny yellow flowers! I could imagine the softness of the dress as I walked into church this summer.

As the peddler set out a bundle of bright woven rag carpets, I couldn't resist touching the tight weave. Mama's crocheted rag rugs were made with a loose stitch. They were not tight like these.

Shiny tins and baskets were stacked in rows inside the cart. The peddler had tin plates and cups, spoons and forks, a basket of marbles, jackknives for the boys, and colorful jump ropes for the girls. So many tempting things to buy!

"Pick out a jackknife," Papa told Charles. "And each of you girls can pick out a pencil." He smiled at Dora and me. "School will be starting again before we know it."

My "maybe" died when I heard those words. I knew a knife was a necessary tool for the men, but it was hard to see my tiny flame of hope for a new dress snuffed out.

I swallowed my disappointment, gave Papa a tiny smile, and chose a pencil. "Put six lemon drops on the bill," Papa added as the peddler tallied our purchases.

A box of nails, pencils for school, one black and one white spool of thread, a tin cup and spoon for Mary, a jackknife for Charles, a small rubber ball for Paul, and lemon drops—that was all we were buying. Dora beamed as she clutched her coveted pencil, and Paul's grin spread from ear to ear as he squeezed the bright red ball between his outstretched hands.

Toys were almost nonexistent in our home. Instead, we children spent a lot of time swinging on our two rope swings, one hanging from a tree limb and the other from the barn rafters. We also played tag, raced just for the fun of running, climbed trees, or used Charles's homemade slingshot to pick off troublesome blackbirds or sparrows. Our active imaginations made good use of every free minute.

When I caught Dora's and Paul's shining eyes, I couldn't help but smile despite my disappointment. Dora started school in the fall, and to her, a pencil was the most important thing she could have received from the peddler. Paul's joy came from the novelty of receiving a simple, store-bought toy.

That evening Charles asked me, "Do you want to help me flush out some gophers tomorrow after dinner?" He opened and closed the sharp, smooth knife blade, and I knew he was itching to use it.

"Sure!" I answered. "That knife ought to finish them off in a hurry. I'm glad Papa let you get one." As I said the words aloud, I found I truly meant them. *After all, our family is rich with laughter even if we dress in flour sacks!*

"Thanks, Anna. I wish you could have gotten something more. Maybe we can get a lot of gophers this summer and you can buy something in town. The Mercantile sells a lot of things."

It made me feel good that Charles cared. He had told me earlier that the municipal office in town was paying two cents for every gopher tail brought to them. Prairie dogs, or gophers, as the locals called them, were pests. This was one way the local leaders encouraged their destruction. These little rodents banded together, digging burrows and tunnels under the ground and mounding up dirt at their entrances. These "prairie dog towns" wrecked farmland and ranches. Horses and cattle could break a leg if they stepped into one of these deep burrows.

The next afternoon Charles and I headed out to the pasture where the gophers were constructing a new "town." We each carried two heavy pails of water, and Charles had a hoe. It was hard work, but the prospect of collecting some gopher tails made it worthwhile. When we reached the "town," we had to be very quiet because gophers have a keen sense of hearing. They disappear into their holes at the first sign of danger.

We stood motionless, waiting for a curious little gopher to pop his head out and scrutinize his surroundings. Once we knew a gopher was in his burrow, we located his exit door, which was a simple hole in the ground some distance from the entry hole. Gophers seemed to use their exit doors only for emergencies.

It wasn't long until a gopher popped up at his entrance

mound. His beady eyes scanned the world around him as he stood on his hind legs and sniffed the air. When he spotted us, he disappeared down his hole. Charles soon found the exit hole and stood with his hoe raised as I dumped a bucket of water into the entry hole. I poured the water in quickly so it wouldn't soak into the dirt. We wanted it to *whoosh* through the tunnel and flush out the gopher.

In a few seconds, the gopher popped out his exit door. *Whack!* The hoe caught him and he lay still. Charles's face sported a huge grin as we moved away from the dead gopher and once again stood like statues, waiting for the next one to appear. It didn't take long before another gopher raised his head. Twice more we successfully executed our maneuvers. But after the third gopher had been killed, the "town" went into high alert. Although we waited motionless in the hot sun for a long time, nothing stirred.

"Six cents! Pretty good for one day!" Charles tossed the tails into an empty bucket, then left the dead gophers at the edge of the field for the vultures to find.

"We should try catching crows," Charles said. "Harley told me they pay the same for a pair of crow's feet."

"How would you catch a crow?" I asked. "That seems impossible."

Sunday morning dawned bright and clear. Heavy dew glistened over the countryside. Crows scolded from the fencerow, and a meadowlark sang. A few fluffy white clouds floated lazily in the deep blue sky. Dressed in our Sunday best, we all climbed aboard the wagon. Down the dirt road the wagon wheels hummed as our lively team trotted in unison.

It was not always possible for us to attend church services because of the twelve miles to travel. The trip took over an hour. In cold winter weather or when it was stormy, we stayed home and had family Sunday school in our living room. It was a disadvantage to live so far from church, but sunny Sundays like today were a wonderful gift.

As soon as Papa parked the wagon in the churchyard, Charles unhitched the team. He led them to the water trough, and once they had a good drink, he tied them to the hitching post. In the meantime, Papa helped Mama and the little ones down from the wagon. We walked around a little, stretching the kinks out of our stiff limbs before heading inside to sit on the hard church benches.

Anna's Courage

"I'm so glad your family could come!" Cousin Edith greeted me inside the little country church house.

"Yes, I'm glad too. I see Irene has already claimed Dora." I smiled at the two little cousins, their heads together as if sharing a deep secret.

"I'm guessing Irene is telling Dora our plans for today. She could hardly get to church fast enough!"

"Oh?" I searched my cousin's beaming face with anticipation.

"We are inviting your family for dinner today!" Edith blurted out, squeezing my arm.

"Good!" I replied, smiling at her. Edith was a year older than I was and my closest girl cousin. Since we lived in different school districts, our times together seemed few and far between. *What is that poem we learned in school? Something about a rare day in June? Well, spending a Sunday afternoon with my cousin is indeed a rare day in June!*

That afternoon we older cousins hiked to Beaverhill Lake, not far from Grandpa King's farm. "I hope you can spend a day with us again when the Saskatoon berries are ripe," Edith remarked. "Look how the bushes are loaded with blooms."

"Oh, I hope so!" I exclaimed. "That would be fun!" I examined the tiny flowers covering the branches. I could almost taste the sweet firmness of the dark, ripe berries.

When we returned to the house, we went indoors to get a cool drink of water. I could hear the men discussing some new machine and heard Grandpa say, "I don't know how a young farmer can get ahead with the low grain prices and the high cost of machinery." He pulled on his beard, deep in thought.

"That's right," Papa agreed. "If nothing changes, we will have to move."

I stopped, frozen by the words. *Move? No, we don't want to move. I like my friends here.* A sense of dread settled in my heart. This was the second time I had heard Papa mention moving.

My thoughts were suddenly interrupted by screams and shrieks from the younger children outside. "The baby fell into the well!" Irene cried, flinging open the screen door. Mama uttered a cry and jumped up so fast her chair fell over backward.

The baby? Our baby! Dear, precious Mary! I hurried after Mama, but she was running so fast I couldn't keep up. Mama nearly flew, her feet hardly touching the ground in her haste to cross the yard. A tight knot of children crouched on the grass.

Reaching the children, Mama fell on her knees, not sure what to expect. Looking down, she saw dear little Mary in a shallow tub of water, wedged tightly against a large can of cream. She was soaking wet and sobbing—but safe. It wasn't a real well Mary had fallen into, but a three-and-a-half-foot hole dug into the ground on the north side of the house. A tub had been set into this hole and filled with water. It was a cool place to store the cream until it could be taken to the train station to be shipped and sold.

Papa quickly pushed past me and lifted out a screaming Mary, handing her to Mama. What a bedraggled sight she was! Her wet clothing clung to her, and water dripped onto Mama as she held Mary close, patting her back and whispering gentle words of comfort.

We all praised God when we returned to the house. We were so thankful it hadn't been the deep well, and that little Mary was only badly frightened.

Everyone was tired when we headed home that evening. I was so glad Mary was with us. But there was also a weight in my chest. *Is Papa really thinking about moving? Surely he is not serious.*

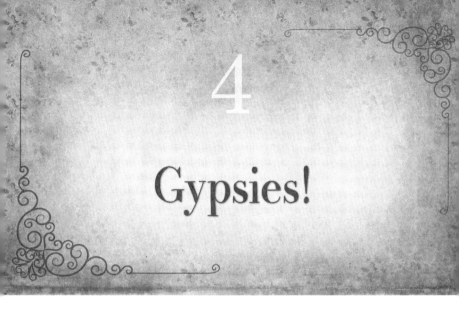

4

Gypsies!

"I think today would be a good day to clean out the barn," Papa announced at the breakfast table. Charles's head came up eagerly.

"Can I drive the horses?" he asked, leaning forward on the bench. At ten years old, he hoped he was old enough to drive the horses to the field without help.

"Ned and Bob would never obey you." The warning tumbled out of my mouth before Papa had time to answer. "You know the trouble Papa had last year."

Mama started chuckling. Papa glanced at her, his own smile widening. Full-blown laughter erupted around the table as Mama started wiping tears. Laughter always made Mama cry. The more she wiped her tears, the harder she laughed. It was a merry-go-round that we children loved to get started.

"What's so funny?" Dora asked, making everyone laugh even more.

"How about a little story to explain why we're laughing?" Papa said. He smiled at Dora and began. "Last summer I started cleaning out the barn just like we are going to do today. Ned and Bob are usually willing workhorses and cooperate well together, but Old Ned does not like to pull a heavy load.

"Last year when I loaded the stoneboat with a full load of manure, the horses did something they had never done before. I had loaded inside the barn like I always do, and the horses passed through the barn door with no trouble. Then they pulled the heavy load across the well-packed barnyard.

"But when I started across the pasture, Old Ned stopped. He refused to take one more step! Bob leaned into his harness, like this." Papa leaned forward in his chair. "But Ned braced his feet like this." And Papa pushed his toes against the kitchen floor.

Dora and Paul started laughing. "Nothing I did would make Ned go," Papa continued. "I talked to him and put pressure on the reins. I even hit his rump with the edge of my pitchfork, but he didn't flinch. Nothing! So I stood on the loaded stoneboat and waited. I figured Ned would move when he got tired of standing.

"Sure enough! All of a sudden I saw Old Ned's ears go back. I jabbed my pitchfork into the load and braced myself as both horses tore off across the pasture." Dora's hand flew to her mouth, and Paul's big brown eyes shone with excitement.

"Well," Papa continued, "the horses soon slowed down to a walk. It was hard work for them to keep running with a full load, but I was throwing the manure off the stoneboat as fast as I could. Ned sensed the load getting lighter, so he kept up a steady walk as I finished unloading."

"Old Ned did that every time Papa pulled out of the barn with a full load!" I said, smiling into Dora's wide, shining eyes.

"Oh!" Paul said. "Ned was very naughty!" The whole family laughed again.

"Can we watch you today, Papa?" Dora begged. "I want to see Ned do it!"

"I guess if Mama agrees," Papa said. "You can watch Charles and me do the first load, but I don't think Ned will be balky this year. At least I hope not. But after the first load, you girls have to come back in and do your morning work."

Mama decided to join us, so we all traipsed outdoors to the corral. We leaned against the fence at the end of the barn and watched Papa and Charles fork manure onto the stoneboat. The stoneboat was a low platform built on wooden runners. A wide board ran across the front, with a peg nailed to the center of the board. Papa wrapped the lines from the horses around this peg.

Slowly the horses moved down the wide aisle in the barn between the pens.

"Giddyap," Papa called. Obediently the horses moved forward, stopping only when Papa called "Whoa." Because the horses obeyed Papa, he could load the stoneboat without having to touch the reins. "Giddyap...whoa...giddyap...whoa," Papa called, and the horses moved through the barn until they reached the big doors that opened to the pasture.

"Will they go?" Dora clasped her hands and held her breath. She seemed torn between wanting them to obey Papa and longing to watch the show if they refused. "I want to see them run, but I don't want Papa or Charles to get hurt."

Ned and Bob leaned into their harnesses as they left the barn. The stoneboat slowed as it hit the pasture, but both horses plodded onward. Out through the pasture the horses pulled the heavy load, with Papa and Charles

Anna's Courage

slinging manure from both sides. "Praise the Lord!" Mama said.

But Dora was disappointed. "That was nothing to watch," she pouted.

"Come, girls. The wash needs to be hung out, the dishes are waiting, and the garden is overrun with weeds! And what are we women doing? Nothing! Doing nothing gets nothing done!" We all laughed. Grabbing Dora's hand, she and I raced ahead to the house.

"What do you think Mama hid this week?" Dora asked as she squeezed the water out of the dusting rag. "I hope it's another button like you found last week. I loved the dark blue center! I hope I find what she hid." Her tone was wistful as she gave her rag a swift shake, fluffing it up before she began wiping away the thick film of dust that blanketed every flat surface. Daily summer winds helped make the heat more bearable, but they also blew thick dust through the open windows and doors.

"Keeping ahead of the dust is just part of a woman's summer work," Mama had told me when I was Dora's age and had complained about having to dust all the time. Then, to make dusting less tedious, Mama had started hiding a little prize somewhere. It might be beneath a doily, under a lamp, or in some corner that would be easy to skip.

The reward for cleaning thoroughly was keeping the item

we found. It might be a pretty stone, a button without a match, a wild rose, a seed pod, or a pussy willow branch. Sometimes Mama hid a note with a special message. It might say we could play in the creek after lunch, have a half hour to read, or take a fresh jug of water out to Papa. We girls loved to seek out these surprises. Dusting became a game instead of drudgery.

I swiped my rag along the window frame, thinking about Shirley's comment that my work would be fun for her. Suddenly I straightened up. *Why, Shirley is right! Mama does make work fun for us!* I smiled as some of Mama's familiar phrases popped into my mind. "Let's hurry!" she would say. "This job won't take long!" Or, "It's not worth doing unless you do your best."

Another favorite was, "Hard work never hurts anyone, but it sure makes you sleep well!" I thought of Mama saying, "Sing while you work. It makes the task fly." It did help to make work go faster, and Mama was always singing! But my favorite saying was, "Money is scarce, but laughter is plenty."

That afternoon I was taking the dry clothes off the line and dropping them into a basket. Suddenly the steady *clip-clop* of plodding horses and the creaking of a wagon floated through the quietness. Turning, I waited to see who was coming up the road. *It must be more than one horse with all that racket!* The nearer the travelers came, the louder became the rumble of wheels, the jangle of harnesses, and the mixed-up rhythm of horses' hooves.

Whoever can it be? I kept one eye on the road while unpinning laundry. My hands stopped when a chimney poked over the hill. Soon a tin wagon roof appeared. Then a lone horse pulling a little house wagon. A man in a straw hat sat on the seat in front, holding the reins, with a colorfully dressed woman beside him. Soon another chimney came into sight.

Gypsies! My eyes swept over the farmyard to make sure none of the little ones were outside. My heart hammered as I stripped the rest of the clothes off the line and darted to the house. I didn't even feel the heavy tub thumping against my shins as it left red bruises. All I could think about was getting out of sight.

"Mama, Gypsies are coming!" I burst through the kitchen door with the heavy tub. But no one was there. The house was silent. I stood still for a minute before it dawned on me that the little ones were napping, and Mama was rocking little Mary. *Whew! That's a relief.* My breathing slowed a bit.

Standing well back from the doorway, I watched the first wagon pass, then the second and the third. And more were coming! Sunlight glinted off the tin roofs, and each wagon seat held at least two people. I saw one woman's dangling earrings swaying with the wagon's motion, and another lady held a baby on her lap. Several dogs trotted behind the wagons, keeping in the shadows. The door to one wagon was fastened back against the side. Two children sat in the doorway with their feet swinging back and forth. More people sat inside.

I counted eight wagons. A shiver ran up my spine. *This must be a big band of Gypsies! How far will they go before they set up camp? Have they seen anything on our farm that they'll come back to steal tonight? Would they have tried to snatch little*

Mary if she had been playing outside?

I had heard that Gypsies were partial to light-skinned, curly-haired children. And I had heard stories of how they came at night and stole chickens, small tools, and even horses. Fear clutched me. I had always been afraid of Gypsies. Then I remembered the Gypsy band that had gone past our farm two years earlier.

I chuckled at the memory, and my fear began to evaporate. I had stayed home one afternoon for an hour or so while everyone else went to the neighbors' place. Greg, a neighbor boy, had come to ask if Mama could help doctor his brother's foot. "He cut it bad with the ax," he had explained.

Papa had the horses hitched to the wagon, so he offered to take Mama over. "Jump in," he called to the younger children. "You may as well ride along."

Papa had been filling the cattle's water trough when Greg arrived. I didn't want to go to the neighbors because all the children were boys, so I asked Papa to let me stay at home and finish pumping the water.

Pumping water was not a hard job. Even though the neighbors lived just down the road, I felt very pleased when the family departed, leaving me, a nine-year-old, at home alone! I chuckled softly at the memory. I had felt very grown-up—until the Gypsies appeared!

I had been standing in the well house, pumping the handle up and down in perfect rhythm when I caught sight of a row of wagon houses traveling the road. They were going right past our farm—and I was at home alone! Without thinking, I scrambled into the rafters of the well house. Papa had laid some boards across the rafters to have a platform on which to keep the pump tools handy. It proved to be the perfect hiding place! Wanting to make sure they would be far away before I came down, I closed my eyes to rest. Within minutes, I was fast asleep.

When my family returned home, they couldn't find me. They called my name and searched the house. No Anna. Charles ran out and checked the barn. No Anna. Papa and Mama became alarmed, as they had seen the Gypsy band pass. Had the Gypsies seen me and coaxed me to ride with them? Should they follow the band and find out? The thought of the Gypsies taking me was not unfounded. Mama and Papa had heard of things like that happening, but Papa would not accuse them without proof.

Papa knew that could be disastrous for the community. Retaliation from the band would be swift and dangerous, and at a time least expected.

But Papa was troubled. Where could Anna be? "Let's pray and ask God to show us what to do or where to look." As Papa gathered the somber family together, Dora started crying and Mama was near tears too.

"Our Father in heaven," Papa had prayed with a tremble in his voice. "You know where Anna is. Show us what we should do. Keep her safe, Lord, and give us wisdom to do the right thing. In your holy name we pray. Amen."

"Are we going after the Gypsies?" eight-year-old Charles asked.

"Let's look around outside again. Maybe we can find some clue that will help us," Papa answered. Everyone followed Papa outdoors. Once more the barn was searched.

Charles looked in the feed room. He didn't really think his sister could hide in a bucket or a feed sack, but he wasn't going to take any chances, so he checked them all.

Papa had stopped in the barnyard. "Mama," he called, "look at the chickens scratching in their pen. The Gypsies did not stop here. They would have taken our chickens. And both pitchforks are in plain sight. Our buckets are all here too. Anna must be somewhere on the farm."

He cupped his hands and called as loud as he could. "Anna! Anna! Yahoo!" The chickens squawked, scattering in every direction.

Suddenly Papa saw bare feet drop down into the doorway of the well house. "Anna!" he sputtered as my faded brown dress came into view. "Why are you in the well house? Why didn't you answer when we called? We have been looking all over for you!"

Still half-asleep, I didn't answer at first.

"What happened, Anna?" Mama put her arm around me. She could see I had been sleeping and was still slightly confused.

"The Gypsies," I stammered. "I-I was pumping water, and I didn't want them to see me, so I hid in the rafters. I guess I fell asleep and didn't hear you come home."

"I was scared," Dora had wailed, throwing her chubby arms around me. It was obvious by the relief on my parents' faces that they had been scared too.

Now, as I watched the Gypsy wagons disappear down the road, I asked myself, *Why am I afraid of Gypsies? They have never done anything to us. It is time to act my age! After all, I am eleven years old. But they do look scary. They have such dark, unsmiling faces. And they look so different with their jewelry and colorful clothing.*

What concerned me the most was that they stole and did not believe in God. But Mama said God loves the Gypsies just as much as He loves us.

A frown shadowed my face as I thought of Papa's warning: "A lot of the stories we hear may not be true, but we still need to be cautious when we see a Gypsy band. We need to be respectful, but we also need to remember that these people do not believe in God. When you see a band coming, the best thing to do is to go inside the house or barn. I want you children to be careful, but I don't want you to be afraid. God has promised to take care of us, and we need to trust Him."

I sighed. It was hard to remember to always trust. It seemed I forgot so often! Carefully I piled the clean clothes onto the table and began to fold them.

"But you have to climb up with me! There is no other way we can rob the crows' nest!" Charles argued as I stood gazing up at the spot he was pointing to. Two crows leered down at us. "See the nest above the fork?"

"Of course I see the nest. It's in plain sight! That's not the problem."

"I've been watching it the last two days," Charles hurried on. "The parents are feeding the babies. If I can get the nest down, we can get all the little birds. Think how many feet that will be! We'll have at least four pairs—maybe five. That would be a whole dime!"

"Are you sure they take baby bird feet?" I asked.

I stared up at the nest sandwiched between two smaller branches. It was close to a larger branch, but I wondered if the branch was thick enough to stand on. And I wasn't sure I wanted the job of fending off a pair of angry crows. Could I hang onto that skinny limb above the nest and swing a stick without falling?

But eight cents! Maybe ten! I juggled the pros and cons before deciding. *I guess eight cents would be enough reward for climbing the tree.* But I didn't feel like giving in to Charles. My job seemed the more difficult of the two. Charles often teased me, and this was a chance to tease him in return. I rarely got such an opportunity.

"Are-you-sure-they-want-baby-feet?" I punctuated each word with as much doubt as I could muster, trying to keep from smiling.

"Anna, baby crows grow up to be big crows! And big crows eat our wheat! Just think! We climb this tree, get four or five babies, climb down, and we're done! It's that easy!"

"Hear, hear. I secede from this argument." I didn't know if Charles knew the meaning of *secede* or not. Smugly I thought of the school history lesson where someone said, "I secede from this political party." I didn't know if I was using the word correctly, but I was withdrawing my argument. With a smile, I began hunting for just the right stick. Charles made no comment, and I knew he was still trying to figure out what secede meant. I studied the sticks lying on the ground. My stick had to be big enough and strong enough to deal out hefty whacks but not too heavy.

"Here is a perfect stick," Charles said as he handed me one. "I'll start up the tree and you follow. When we get to that big branch, you keep the adult birds away while I grab the nest. You may have to slide past me. We won't know until we get up there."

Before we had climbed even halfway up the tree, the parent crows sensed trouble coming and began an awful racket, screaming as they swooped back and forth above our heads.

"Keep coming," Charles encouraged when I hung back. "They always make a lot of noise. They won't hurt you." Trying to be brave, I kept climbing. I soon noticed that even though we were getting closer to the nest, the birds were not coming any closer to us.

I hope Charles is right, I thought as several other crows joined in the ruckus. "*Caw, caw, caw,*" they screamed. Their wings flapped, their sharp beaks threatened, and their beady eyes stared at us ferociously as they swooped and circled.

"They're furious, Charles!" I hollered above the din. "I think they're calling us every name they can think of!"

"Be ready! The nest is just above us," he called back.

I edged past him onto the branch that had looked pretty thick from the ground, but now it seemed weak and skinny

as it swayed under my weight. I
held my breath as I inched
along, hanging on for dear
life to the spindly branch
overhead. Desperately
I swung my stick back
and forth.

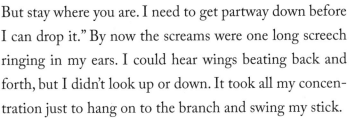

"Keep the birds back!"
Charles said tersely. "I'm
getting the nest…Got it!
But stay where you are. I need to get partway down before
I can drop it." By now the screams were one long screech
ringing in my ears. I could hear wings beating back and
forth, but I didn't look up or down. It took all my concen-
tration just to hang on to the branch and swing my stick.

"Okay!" Charles called. "You can come down!" I dropped
my stick and scrambled down the tree so fast I didn't even
notice when my dress caught on a branch and ripped. Once
I was on the ground, my legs turned to jelly, and I sank into
a heap.

"Four baby crows! Eight cents! Whee!" Charles whistled.
"That was fun!"

When I didn't answer, he said, "It's good you have a lot
of courage." Then he added with a saucy grin, "For a girl."

Once I had caught my breath, it didn't seem quite so

bad. The birds hadn't touched me, and it hadn't taken very long. And eight cents made it worth the scare. Charles was right; this was far easier than hunting gophers. We had spent over an hour in the hot sun getting six cents' worth of gopher tails, while today we had earned eight cents in less than ten minutes!

But courage? Charles could think what he wanted— my legs were still weak. It was certainly not courage that had made me hang on. My inner shaking could better be described as fear, terror, or even panic. But not courage.

5

A Scary Bull

Once the hot days of summer arrived, so did the mosquitoes. I had forgotten the misery they brought when no breeze swept across the yard or fields. On these hot, still days, the leaves on our cottonwood trees hung dull and listless under the scorching sun. Even the branches of the tall evergreen trees stood stiff and silent instead of whispering their restful music. It seemed the only sound that filled the outdoors was the high-pitched whine from hordes of mosquitoes blanketing the countryside. The screens on the windows and doors became black with the whining insects as they fought for an opportunity to slip indoors.

"It doesn't matter to a mosquito if they are drawing blood from a human or an animal," Papa said one evening as we sat at the supper table, trying to tune out the ever-present hum of these uninvited guests. "All they are interested in is feasting." He slapped his arm, leaving a smudge of red where a mosquito had been.

"Where do they come from?" Dora asked, brushing one away from her neck.

"We just have them. It's summertime," Charles said matter-of-factly.

"Yes, they are a part of summer, just like flies, the green grass, the warm sun, and the weeds," Papa said. "Summer brings us things we like—and also things we have to put up with. The creek and the thick woods surrounding our fields are good places for mosquitoes. They thrive in the marshes around Beaverhill Lake. In fact, this whole area is ideal for mosquitoes."

"I like having woods and a creek on our farm, but I don't like mosquitoes," Dora sighed.

"I hate them too," I said, slapping one on her back. "That's one less to get you tonight," I told her when she winced.

I thought about the mosquitoes. Some mornings when we went outdoors, we were greeted by droves of them rising out of the dewy grass as we walked. We knew then that we were in for a long, unpleasant day. On those days, Papa would dress with care before he left the house. He would put on a straw hat with a thin mesh cloth hanging from the outer edge. A drawstring ran around the bottom of this cloth. He turned up his shirt collar, put the mesh cloth over his collar, then pulled the drawstring tight. With his shirt collar inside the mesh cloth, it was impossible for any mosquitoes to get inside.

Next he would make sure his pant legs went over the top of his boots. After that was done, he tucked his long shirtsleeves into work gloves. It always made me hot and itchy to see Papa dressed up like that. I felt sorry for him. Summer was hot enough without adding extra layers. No wonder his hair was dripping with sweat when he came in for dinner!

"How can you stand to work outdoors with all those hot clothes?" Charles wondered.

"It's either that or be eaten alive," Papa said.

The mosquitoes disappeared when it became windy. *Would it be wrong to pray for wind every day?* I wondered. I would have to ask Mama if that was a selfish prayer. *But how can it be selfish if it would help Papa?*

I not only felt sorry for Papa but also for our workhorses. On days when the mosquitoes were thick, Papa put a canvas basket over the horses' faces to keep them away. The horses also had to fight biting flies. While they were working in the fields, they were constantly stamping their feet or switching their tails in an effort to keep the pests at bay. By the time they came in from the field, the poor horses were jumpy and dripping with perspiration. Charles would run out and help Papa unhitch them, as they were too restless to stand still.

One of the jobs Charles and I did each evening when the mosquitoes were out was to prepare smudge pots for the animals. We each grabbed an old pail and put a bit of dry straw in the bottom. We lit the straw, then after it had burned a little, we placed some damp straw on top. This caused a long, smoky burn that the mosquitoes hated. If the cattle stood or lay in the smoke drift, the insects would leave them alone. When the horses and cattle were turned out into the pasture for the night, we followed them with our smoking pails.

Bringing in the cows when the air was thick with mosquitoes was not a pleasant task either. This was another of our daily jobs. One person brought the cows in from the pasture and drove them down the road to the yard gate. The other person stood by the gate to make sure the cows turned in instead of going on past.

Fighting the mosquitoes while waiting at the yard gate was far from pleasant. No amount of slapping, arm-swinging, turning circles, feet-stamping, or any other acrobatics kept the pests away. The whining, biting mob came right back.

The only thing I dreaded more than fighting the

mosquitoes was bringing in the cows when the bull was in the pasture. When that happened, my imagination went wild. I was afraid the bull would come up behind me and start pawing, bellowing, and snorting.

I knew I couldn't complain to Papa again about my fear because the bull had never bothered us. When I had told him I didn't like the bull, he had looked surprised. "Carry a stick with you," he told me. "And don't act scared. The bull is young and won't hurt you. He won't bother you if you go calmly about your work."

"I hate that bull!" I told Charles one evening when we went to bring in the cows. Suddenly I had an idea. "Hey, Charles," I said. "I can watch the gate if you bring in the cows." *Even if the mosquitoes are ferocious, it's better than going into the pasture with the bull*, I thought.

Charles looked at me and shrugged. "I guess we could do that. I'm not scared of the bull. He's just half grown."

"I know, but he still scares me," I confessed. I sighed with relief that Charles finally knew how I felt. But I didn't tell him that I sometimes had nightmares of the bull chasing me. I always woke up just before the bull reached me. It was just a dream, but it was so real it always took a while for my fear to subside. It seemed I could almost feel his hot breath on the back of my neck.

If only Mama and Papa knew how much courage it takes for me to bring in the cows! I would wail to myself. But I was ashamed to let them know. *Anna,* I would sternly tell myself, *stop being afraid! The bull is not big yet.* I hated having this fear, but I did not know how to get over it.

Now the problem was solved. *If Charles has the courage to go alone, I will gladly endure the mosquitoes.*

By mid-July, the green bean plants were heavy with beans and blooms, promising a bumper crop. "Praise God from whom all blessings flow!" Mama sang as her hoe pulled loose garden dirt up against the potato plants in quick, even strokes. She noticed a horse and buggy turn in our lane and stopped singing. Shielding her eyes against the morning sun, Mama tried to see who it was. Then she laid down her hoe between the dirt ridges of the potato hills.

"I think it's Mrs. Welsh coming for beans. I left a message

at the store saying we had extra beans for sale." I could hear happiness in Mama's words.

"Come in with me and take a little break," Mama called as she started for the house.

"I hope she buys a lot of beans!" I murmured. "We could sure use the money!" I thought of the things we needed before school started. I hoped I could get more than just a new pencil!

Mrs. Welsh parked her horse and buggy beside the barn. She looped the reins loosely over the buggy's front, leaving her mare to stand without being tied, then walked up the path to meet my mother. This practice was not uncommon if the driver planned to return shortly, and this horse looked as if Mrs. Welsh had done it many times. The mare stood quietly, with only an occasional toss of her head to rid herself of some pesky insect. Or maybe she was just letting everyone know she was patiently waiting!

I smiled to myself and felt glad to be alive on this lovely day. I rejoiced in the blue skies overhead and the brisk wind that swept the mosquitoes away. Yes, it was truly a perfect day!

"Mama, shall I swing Mary?" I called as the two women walked to the garden. "Maybe she will go to sleep if I do."

Mama nodded. Mary had been fussy all day, and Mama thought she was cutting a tooth. Back and forth, back and forth, I pushed the rope swing with my toes. Holding Mary snugly against my chest, I hummed softly. Suddenly I was jerked out of my reverie by the snorting of Mrs. Welsh's mare.

The horse was tossing her head again. But this time, her nostrils flared and she pranced backward a few steps before taking off at a run, circling around the barnyard. Then down the lane she tore, her hooves pounding the ground—the empty buggy bouncing along behind. She galloped out through the lane gate, just missing the corner fencepost. Veering to the left, she plunged straight for the barbed wire fence beside the road.

My heart was pounding as hard as the horse's hooves. I wanted to run out to the road and stop the horse, but there was nothing I could do, for Mary had fallen asleep. I craned my neck and saw the little mare swerve. It looked like she might turn and come back, but the buggy wheel caught the barbed wire fence. She stumbled but kept going, ripping off a strip of fence. By this time, Mrs. Welsh and Mama were running down the road. My pent-up breath escaped when Mama caught hold of the bridle and brought the horse to a halt.

It took a little while for them to disentangle the buggy wheel from the barbed wire and lead the mare back to the house. I found out later that several hundred feet of fence

A Scary Bull

had been torn loose in her wild dash!

When the buggy was once more parked beside the barn, the little mare stood heaving and dripping wet, her muscles quivering. "I'm so glad it wasn't worse," Mama said between breaths. "It may have been a horsefly bite that scared her, but we'll never know. I'm thankful no one was hurt, and your horse and buggy seem to be okay."

"I have learned my lesson!" Mrs. Welsh exclaimed. "Never again will I leave my horse untied! I think I'm trembling as bad as she is!" Mrs. Welsh took her handkerchief and wiped the perspiration from her flushed face.

"Come in and rest a little," Mama invited. "I'll get us each a drink of water." I followed them indoors, still carrying the sleeping Mary. Laying her in her crib, I closed the door and slipped back outside. As I surveyed the damaged fence, I pictured again Mrs. Welsh's horse in mad flight down the lane.

I chuckled when I remembered an earlier horse experience. Honey had acted exactly the opposite of the little mare today!

"Honey is the perfect name for this docile old buckskin horse," Papa had assured us when he brought home the sandy-colored horse with a black tail and mane.

One evening Papa had surprised Charles and me by asking, "How would you like to ride Honey to school tomorrow morning?"

"By ourselves?" I asked.

"Sure, you can do it," Papa told us.

"Honey won't hurt a fly," Papa had assured Mama when she voiced concern about us riding the three miles to school alone.

The next morning we set off, excitedly waving goodbye to Mama, Dora, and Paul, all watching from the doorway. It seemed even more thrilling when we could no longer see our house and barn. How grown-up we felt as we rode down the road on our horse with his flowing black mane and tail!

Before long we saw a hawk glide overhead. Then several gophers popped up out of their burrows, sat up on their hind legs, and watched us go past. Honey didn't even notice them. He just kept up a steady *clop, clop, clop* as we neared the big slough and the field where Papa was working.

We heard ducks quacking before we saw them and were thrilled to see a mother duck swimming away with her little ducklings trailing behind. We paid no attention to the saucy crows making their usual ruckus.

When we arrived at the slough, Honey decided he needed a drink. He turned off the road and stepped right into the water! "Honey!" I scolded, slapping his side. "Giddyap! Giddyap!" But Honey acted deaf. He got a drink but then refused to move. "Honey!" I shouted, flicking the reins again. But Honey was where he wanted to be. He kept his feet in the water as though he intended to stay there all day.

"Charles! We'll be late for school! What should we do?" I was nearly in tears. Why did Honey have to be so stubborn? Taking the end of the reins, Charles whacked him hard on the rump. Nothing happened. Finally Charles slid off his back and tried to lead Honey back to the road.

"Anna! He's just standing here with his eyes closed!" Charles cried. Again he pulled on the bridle, but Honey refused to budge. Charles yelled and waved his arms, but Honey didn't even blink.

"Great! A dreaming horse!" I muttered. Charles started laughing, but I didn't think it was funny.

"Well, we had better do something or we'll be here all day." Charles tried pushing Honey's leg, but Honey only lifted it a little and then settled it back into the water.

We knew Papa was working our neighbor's field on the other side of the slough. He had said he would watch for us when we passed. We could hear the jingle of the four-horse team he was using, but we could not see him. There was nothing to do but go tell him. Charles took off running around the slough, while I prepared myself for a long wait.

"Honey, how can you be so mean?" I whacked his neck, tired of just sitting when we should almost be at school. How embarrassing it would be to ride into the schoolyard late on a horse! Suddenly I saw Papa and Charles emerge from the tree line.

"Papa was at this end of the field!" Charles panted as they reached me. "He tied up the horses and came right away."

"Climb up behind Anna," Papa told Charles as he took hold of the bridle. Honey opened his eyes, then his ears perked up and he tossed his head. He looked straight at Papa.

"Hold the reins like this," Papa told me as he showed the proper tightness for holding the lines. "You shouldn't have any more trouble if you hold them taut. Let Honey know you mean business." Little crinkles appeared at the corners of his eyes as he smiled. "Giddyap!" he called out as he swatted Honey's rump. Another swat followed, and Honey stepped out of the water and onto the road. He didn't stop until we reached the hitching post at school.

School had already started, and I felt mortified to come in late. I could just imagine the boys hooting when they heard what happened. The boys did laugh, but I decided I would not let it bother me; I would simply laugh with them.

Once again one of Mama's sayings gave me courage: "Laugh at yourself and laugh *with* others, but never laugh *at* others."

6

Tired of Working?

One summer day seemed to flow into the next. July sped past, and we were well into August, but there was no slowdown in our work. *I'm so tired!* I thought. *Bone weary.* I let out a sigh as I pushed a strand of damp hair off my forehead.

A smile spread across my face as I pictured my weary bones talking to each other. "More work?" my leg bones protested to my arm bones. "I've been walking miles today!"

"If you think walking is hard work, try pushing that wheelbarrow load of beans!" the arm bones replied. "You get to rest far more than we do!"

"I have something to tell you both!" my stiff backbone

interrupted. "Try stooping over for half the day in the garden! Now that is something worth complaining about!" I chuckled at the imaginary conversation.

Mama smiled at me as she used the corner of her apron to wipe her hot, steamy face. Lifting a jar of boiling beans out of the canner, she carried it to the table. Holding a rag for protection, she flipped the jar upside down and placed it on its top. Four more times Mama returned to the table, each time adding another jar to the rows cooling on a thick cloth. As soon as the canner was empty, Mama put in the

last full jars. She added more wood to the stove, then wiped her face again.

Mama sure looks hot and tired! Does she ever wish we didn't have so much work to do? The thought startled me. Why, Mama was always working! Cleaning, baking, sewing, patching—whether indoors or out—she was always doing something! She often sang as she worked. And she laughed with us and told us stories. I frowned in contemplation. *Does Mama really like to work all the time?*

"Are we done with beans for this year?" I asked.

"Yes, we are!" Mama beamed. "We have certainly been blessed with a bumper crop! We have all we need, and Mrs. Welsh got all she wanted. We could even give the Jordan family a nice amount."

"I'm so hot!" I said. I twisted my damp braids around and around my head. What I longed to say was, "Mama! I'm tired of working!" I wanted to groan when I thought of all the extra chores of summer—the never-ending hoeing, picking, and canning jar after jar of garden vegetables. With all our canning and baking, the kitchen hadn't cooled off all summer!

Without looking at the clock, I knew it would take the rest of the afternoon to finish our household tasks, and then it would be chore time. We would have to bring in the cows and milk them, wash the cream separator and milk buckets, gather the eggs, feed the animals, fill the wood box, carry in water, fry potatoes for supper, and wash the dishes. It wore me out just thinking about it!

I thought of Shirley. What did she do all day? It had never worked for her to come spend a day, but I couldn't imagine her thinking all this work was fun. *Maybe, just maybe, this fall she could come out and see how much "fun" our work is!*

"Mama," I blurted out. "Don't you ever get tired of working?"

Mama looked at me in surprise. "What a strange question!" she said. Then she chuckled as she looked at the messy kitchen floor, the dirty pots and pans, and the dry clothes flapping on the line outside. "I actually do," she said. "I get hot and tired. But I would be sad if there was no work to do."

I must have looked confused, because she added, "I'll explain what I mean once the wash is brought in. You and Dora run out and do that while I clean up this canning mess. Folding clothes will give us a good time to talk."

Dora and I hurried to do our job, both of us eager to hear what Mama had to say. We knew it would likely contain a story. We hoped it would be one we hadn't heard before!

"It was the first summer we were married," Mama began as she picked up a shirt. Laying it flat on the table, she dipped her fingers into a bowl of water and shook some water droplets over the shirt. Rolling up the shirt, she laid it aside. This was the start of her ironing pile. Cotton clothes were notoriously wrinkled after washing. Dampening them made the task of ironing much easier.

"Papa had all his crops planted, and I had a garden started. Everything was growing well, and we had high hopes for the little farm we had rented. We didn't have much, just the bare essentials to farm with, but we were young and strong."

Then Mama turned to Dora. "Do you remember when my birthday is?" she asked.

"You just had your birthday!" Dora said.

"Yes, I did. It was three weeks ago, on July 12. Do you remember how warm it was on my birthday and what we did?"

"We went to the lake near Grandpa's place and ate a picnic lunch," Dora answered, her face lighting up.

"I'm going to tell you what happened on my birthday that year. It was before Papa and I had any of you children.

"The night before my birthday I went to bed very pleased. I had saved enough cream to make a cake for myself as a surprise I would share with Papa. We didn't have eggs to spare, but there was cream. It was nippy outdoors that night, but we gave it little thought. You know how it can get pretty cold at night even if it is hot during the day." I nodded and smoothed out a flour-sack tea towel before folding it.

"We woke up shivering the next morning. 'It feels more

like fall than summer,' Papa commented as he went to start the fire in the cookstove before leaving the house to do the chores. I dressed quickly and was warming up by the stove when Papa came back into the house, calling my name. His voice sounded funny, and I wondered if something terrible had happened in the barn.

"Had our cow died? I felt panicky when Papa didn't even give me a chance to put on a coat but steered me outdoors without saying anything. I remember gasping at the sight that met my eyes! My heart sank to the bottom of my toes. I felt like crying, and I knew Papa felt the same way. But crying did not fix anything. By now, fingers of early-morning light were spreading across the sky."

I had gotten so caught up in the story that I forgot to keep folding clothes until Mama stopped talking. Guiltily I grabbed another piece. I had forgotten Mama's rule: no stories if they kept you from working!

Mama continued, "Our summer world of green had turned white with glittering frost. There would be no garden—no crops. Nothing for all the months of hard work. It had frosted so hard that Papa found a skim of ice on the chickens' outdoor water trough."

"Oh, Mama, what did you do?" I interrupted. Just hearing Mama talk about it made me feel awful. No wonder Mama had wanted to cry.

Mama only smiled as she resumed her story. "Later that day the sun shone bright and hot. In the days that followed, the whole countryside stank of rotting grain and gardens. Our world looked bleak. What would we do about the farm payment? Our landlord expected us to pay the rent after we harvested our crop of oats and wheat.

"But to answer your question, Anna, of what we did that morning. Well, Papa had his normal chores to do. He had a cow to milk, a pig to feed, and a hungry team of horses in the barn. I made porridge and toasted bread for breakfast. When we sat down to eat, I could tell Papa was worried, but he gave me his usual smile and opened his Bible just as if it were a normal morning. Girls, that impressed me! Papa could have come into the house and started complaining. He could have refused to eat. Instead, his actions showed me he trusted God.

"That morning Papa began reading at Matthew 6:25: 'Therefore I say unto you, Take no thought for your life, what ye shall eat, or what ye shall drink; nor yet for your body, what ye shall put on. Is not the life more than meat, and the body than raiment?'

"By the time Papa got to the end of the chapter, I knew I did not need to worry. God knew our needs and would take care of us if we trusted Him. We did the best we could that summer. The oats were only hulls, and the wheat was straw. We had planned to fatten our hog and slaughter it for winter food, but without good feed the pig did not grow well. When we finally butchered the skinny thing, I got only two-thirds of a gallon of lard. That fall we had to move to another place, as Papa could not pay the rent.

"The house we found to rent had only two rooms, and our drinking water had to be hauled two and a half miles from a creek. But that is another story! We must put these clothes away before Anna needs to bring in the cows!

"But, Anna, back to your first question. Did I answer it?"

I frowned, trying to remember what I had asked. *Oh! Did Mama ever get tired of working?* I shot her a glance. "Sort of," I giggled. "But the story wasn't long enough!"

Mama laughed. "Tomorrow is another day, with just as many hours and just as much work!"

"Thanks, Mama. I can't wait to hear more stories. Is that a new saying you have learned?"

"I just made it up, so it should be new!" Laughter filled the kitchen as I handed little Mary's clothes to Dora and got a stack for myself. *Really,* I thought, *I don't feel so tired anymore!* I thought of all the jars in the basement. We wouldn't go hungry this winter; that was certain! In my mind, I could see row after row of beans and peas. In rows marching along the shelves were other jars filled with fruit from our rhubarb plants, our plum trees, and the wild Saskatoon berry bushes. Jars of wild strawberries and blueberries were not as plentiful but still enough for special occasions.

Once fall arrived, one bin in the coolest part of the basement would be full of carrots buried in sand, and another would hold potatoes. Braids of onions would dangle from the rafters, and the gallon crocks would be full of fried sausage patties sealed in lard. My mouth watered at the thought. They were my favorite! And if that were not enough, red beets, corn, and pumpkins still waited to be harvested and canned. *I think I understand now why Mama doesn't mind work,* I mused. *And I think I might be leaning that way myself!*

"Come on, boss! Shoo, boss!" I called to the cows as I clapped my hands behind them, sending them on the path toward home. Charles was busy helping Papa, and with the bull no longer in the pasture, I loved bringing in the cows!

As I followed the cows to the barn, I remembered the question I had wanted to ask Mama. *Is it selfish to pray and ask God to send wind to keep the mosquitoes away?* Deep down I knew what her answer would be. She would say we need to trust God and accept what He sends. I could hear her say, "Anna, God did not tell us He would make our life easy, but He did tell us to be thankful in everything!"

7

A Day to Remember

"Paul, you will have to play with Mary today. Remember that I told you I am going to school?" Dora's words drifted in from outdoors. I peeked out the kitchen door to see my sister place both hands on Paul's shoulders. "Paul, Mama told me we can play in the hayloft when I get home from school. You can watch for me."

"In the loft!" Paul's sparkly brown eyes were as bright as his sister's. If he and Dora could play in the loft afterwards, he didn't mind if she went to school! Nothing could match the sheer fun of jumping from the huge mountain of hay and plunging to the bottom. Or swinging back and forth on the long rope swing.

I smiled at their excitement. *Good for you, Dora! I'm glad you are making Paul happy before we go to school. Mama has been worried about him.* I wanted to go out and tell Dora how proud I was of her, but I didn't. Instead, I picked up the tin lunch pail that held our dinner. Slices of thick bread spread with butter and mashed hard-boiled eggs made up the special lunch for the three of us on our first day of the new school term.

"Mama, Paul is going to be fine!" I shared. "Dora promised him they would play in the hayloft when she comes home. She even told him he could watch for her!"

"Bless her!" Mama said. "Giving Paul something to look forward to will make the day go faster for him."

Two weeks after school started, Papa went to town to get a part for his swathing machine. When he returned, he brought not only the part but also a forty-pound box of apples he had purchased for a dollar.

"Apples, apples, from the tree. Apples, apples, one, two, three. How many apples will it be? One, two, three…" I chanted a made-up rhyme as I pretended to jump rope around the wooden crate filled with the rare treat for our family.

"Are these all for us?" Paul gaped at the red apples peeking through the slats. He had never seen so many apples.

"Papa, my tummy is hungry!"

Papa patted Paul's head. "Yes, these apples are all for us, but we will let Mama take care of them because we want them to last as long as possible."

He turned to Mama. "Where do you want them?"

"Upstairs," Mama promptly replied. "Let's put them on the empty cot at the head of the stairs. I believe that will be the best place to store them. It's a cool spot tucked under the eaves, and it's out of the way and off the floor."

"What a treasure!" I said as I helped Mama gently transfer the apples to the cot. I breathed in the sweet aroma.

"Yes, it's a rich treasure for all of us to enjoy," Mama agreed. "If we each eat only half an apple a day, we can enjoy them for quite a while."

"Just half of one?" Charles groaned. "I could eat two or three right now!"

I agreed. My mouth watered just looking at them. It was always a treat when we received a package of dried apples from Papa's relatives in Ontario. Mama would pass out one little slice of chewy apple at a time to make them last longer, and now she was going to do the same with these crisp, fresh apples.

"We are not pigs, Charles!" Dora informed him in a prim voice.

"I bet you wish you could eat a whole apple yourself!" he

shot back. Dora wilted. Clearly she had been thinking the same thing I had—*only half an apple at a time?*

"Children," Mama chided, "I know it looks like a lot of apples, but if everyone eats a whole apple every day, we will soon empty this cot. Come, chores are waiting. But who would like a taste of apple before we start work?"

"Apples, apples, on the tree. Apples, apples, one, two, three. How many apples will it be?" I sang as we clomped downstairs.

"Half of one!" Dora cried, and we all burst out laughing.

On Saturday morning we woke to dripping rain. "No field work today." Papa blew on a spoonful of porridge before giving it to Mary. "Open wide!" he said.

"I think today would be a good time to get the barn ready for winter. We need to fix the north wall. I noticed some of the boards are loose. We don't want snow blowing into those pens."

"I plan on melting lard today," Mama said. "It's turning rancid, so I need to heat it to take away the stale taste. I think I will do it in the oven while the bread rises. That will keep the top of the stove free. Anyone hungry for doughnuts?"

"Yes!" Charles shouted, and we all cheered.

Spoons clattered against bowls as we finished our breakfast.

Warmth radiated from the cookstove. A log snapped as it settled firmly into the hot coals. Steam escaped from the teakettle, and rain pattered against the windowpanes. A steady flow of roof water poured into the rain barrel at the corner of the porch, adding its rushing murmur to the sounds of the kitchen.

"It sounds like we have our work cut out for us this morning," Papa smiled. He reached for his Bible on the nearby shelf. Saturday was our special day. It was the only day of the week we didn't have to hurry to get ready for school or church. On Saturdays we changed our Bible reading and prayer to the morning instead of evening because Saturday evenings were always full of preparations for Sunday.

My mind was only partly listening to Papa. I was thinking of our first days of school. Shirley had begged to come out some Saturday. And Harley hadn't changed over the summer—at least not for the better.

Suddenly I sat up straight. I needed to give Papa's words my full attention. "Be careful for nothing," he was reading, "but in everything by prayer and supplication with thanksgiving let your requests be made known unto God. And the peace of God, which passeth all understanding, shall keep your hearts and minds through Christ Jesus."

Papa looked at us children. "These two verses in Philippians 4 are good ones to memorize and remember. Worry never helps us. Let me read them again." This time I really listened to Papa.

I need to pray more and be more thankful, I chided myself. *Too often I don't want to trust God.* Little did I know how my trust would be tested before the day ended.

Mama rose from the table after prayer to add more wood to the fire in the cookstove. I followed her, dipping hot water from the reservoir for the dishes. Hot steam rose as I poured it into the dishpan.

"Mama, may I get water from the rain barrel?" I asked, seeing the empty water pail beside the stove. "It would be easier than going out to the pump in this rain."

"Sure," Mama answered. "Papa said it rained all night, and it hasn't stopped yet."

I picked up the pail and hurried outside to the corner of the porch where rain was gushing into the rain barrel. Our house did not have any spouting, so Papa had made something that worked fairly well. Wooden brackets were nailed to the side of the house just below the roofline. These brackets were placed on a slight downward slant with boards fastened to them. When it rained, the boards caught the roof runoff, funneling most of the water into the barrel.

I peered into the barrel, happy to see the waterline edging closer to the top. If it rained all day, we could use all the water we needed and still have enough in the barrel for baths and hair washing. *What luxury!* I mused as I dipped my pail into the barrel. *Water right outside the house!* I paused for a moment, trailing my fingers in the cool water, reluctant to return to the work waiting in the house.

But suddenly, shaking the water from my fingers, I gave myself a good scolding. "Now get busy! If you don't, the dishwater will be cold!" Lifting out the overflowing pail, I made my way back to the kitchen.

I entered the kitchen just as Mama slid the large, black cast-iron pan full of old, hardened lard into the oven. The pan was almost as wide as the oven door and a good three to four inches deep. "I'll be glad when this job is done," Mama remarked as she shut the oven door. "I hope this will give us enough lard until we do the fall butchering."

Picking up a chunk of home-made soap, I methodically rubbed it over the dishrag. Having Uncle David's family come to help with butchering was the highlight of fall. Butchering was hard work, but with everyone pitching in, we children always found time to snatch a few minutes of play.

A smile tugged at the corners of my mouth. Butchering day never lasted long enough. Playing brief games of "Andy Over" was great fun. The tricky part of the game was to run in the opposite direction from the opposing team after they caught the ball. You did not want to get caught by your opponents. Playing a simple game like this added excitement to the day.

I knew Papa and Uncle David needed to finish the harvest before they did the butchering. It also had to be cold enough to freeze the hanging meat, but I hoped winter wouldn't come as early as it did last year! Butchering day was forgotten as I relived last year's brutal winter months while I washed the dishes. The memories made me shiver.

Our home had been nothing more than a shack. The house we now lived in seemed almost like a mansion in comparison. Though it was unpainted and certainly didn't look like a mansion, it was by far the best house we had ever lived in.

Last year Papa's crops had not yielded enough to cover the rent payments. Because of that, we had to leave the farm and move into a dirty, neglected building that had been sitting empty. Though our landlord had called it a house, it was just a shed with one end partitioned off into a small room. The building had a long, slanting roof, unfinished wood floors, and nothing but outside siding boards to keep out the weather.

Mama had done her best to make it feel like home. She learned that we could get free rolls of brown paper from the elevator, so she got enough to cover all the walls, nailing it up like wallpaper.

She had said it "transformed the place," and it did. The dark, rough, wooden walls were hidden behind the paper, giving the inside a clean, fresh look. Once curtains and pictures were hung and rugs were scattered on the floor, it had seemed like home. But even so, the eight months we had lived there had been an endless endurance of cold, cold, and more cold.

Glancing up from the dishpan, I saw the same flour-sack kitchen curtains that had hung in last winter's house. And the same rugs were on the floor—but what a different floor! The rough floors at the shed-house had been impossible to clean until Mama had the idea of oiling them with a mixture of paraffin wax and coal oil.

My nose wrinkled as I recalled the smelly, hot liquid. We had covered every inch of the floor with the mixture. The hot coal oil had soaked into the boards while the wax remained on top, leaving a smooth sheen when it cooled and dried. This had made it possible to clean the floors fairly well. But it was nothing like the smooth linoleum floors we now had. With that came another thought. *Will we soon have to move?*

What did Papa mean?

"Anna? Why are you just holding your hands in the water?" Dora poked my arm. I jumped, startled to realize that all the dishes had been washed.

"Well!" I sputtered. "They must have washed themselves!" I grinned as Dora's mouth fell open.

"Dishes can't wash themselves!" she exclaimed. A frown puckered her forehead as she looked up into my face.

"No, they can't," I said. "I was just teasing. My mind wasn't paying attention when I washed the dishes. I was thinking of our old house and the two-and-a-half-mile walk Charles and I had to school last winter. It's a good thing you were too young to go to school."

"Why?" Dora's frown deepened. "You said I would like school—and I do!"

"Yes, I'm glad you like school. I am just glad you didn't go last year." How could I tell her how awful it had been to walk to school in thin rubber boots? My feet had often been nearly frostbitten by the time I arrived.

Dora had no idea what chilblains were. Even Mama didn't know how much I had suffered from frostbite. I had been afraid she would make me stay at home if she knew, so I had decided it was better to suffer in silence.

By the time I had arrived at school, my feet often felt like blocks of ice. As they warmed up, it was impossible not to rub my feet together to relieve the burning itch. Rubbing them caused my feet to become so inflamed and tender that I thought I couldn't bear it. But somehow I had to! Like Mama always said, "This too shall pass!"

But I hoped Dora never, ever had to find out what chilblains were.

"All I had to wear was rubber boots, and they didn't keep my feet warm," I explained. "They kept my feet dry, but they didn't protect against the cold. My boots were too small to wrap rags around my feet and still fit. I'm glad we now have nice warm boots to walk to school."

Dora's eyes widened, and she nodded her head.

"Mama, aren't you glad we are living in this house?" I asked as I wiped up the water that had splashed out of the dishpan.

"Yes," Mama answered. "God has given us more than we deserve." She sprinkled flour on the table before lifting out the ball of sweet dough from the pan. Gently she patted and stretched the dough until it lay flat, about a half-inch thick. Taking a sharp knife, she made long, even, diagonal slashes across the dough. "I know we had a hard winter last year, but I was thankful for the roof God provided."

"Even though it leaked?"

"Yes, even with all its leaks," Mama smiled. "I was just thankful to have a leak-free spot large enough to set our beds under! That helped us get through the winter." Mama began cutting the dough in the opposite direction of the previous cuts. "I feel richly blessed to live in this snug home. I don't believe we will have to worry about snow drifting in through the cracks this winter."

Snug—that's the word I wanted! It describes our house perfectly.

"Or frost in the corners and on nail heads," I added. Then I asked, "Why don't you make doughnuts with holes in the middle? Verna's mother does."

"I don't have to turn these," Mama explained as she took a corner of dough to the stove and dropped it into the pan of heating lard. "These are also faster to cut, and you don't have scraps to deal with. And they taste just as good!"

"Maybe so," I said. "But the holes make them look nice."

"Yes, round doughnuts with holes are pretty," Mama replied. "But I don't have time to do something just for looks. Let's be thankful for square ones. I hadn't planned on making doughnuts today, but between the rain and my wanting to melt the lard, I thought I had enough time."

"I like them just how Mama makes them," Dora declared staunchly.

"So do I," I agreed, tweaking Dora's braid. Our doughnuts were not really square—more of a diamond shape—and they tasted every bit as good as those with holes. Once the doughnuts were fried to a golden brown on one side, the light, crispy pointed corners of the dough automatically flipped them onto their uncooked sides.

"Our doughnuts almost fry themselves," I said. "All we do is put the squares into the lard, and then take them out when they're done!" I sniffed the mouth-watering aroma filling the kitchen.

But someday I want to make the other kind. The stubborn thought persisted as I carried the dirty dishwater outdoors and flung it onto the grass. Rain continued to fall, and the runoff from the roof fell *plunk, plunk, plunk* into the water barrel. I liked the sound. It had a comforting rhythm.

My stomach rumbled as I went back inside. *If these dough-nuts were big round ones with holes, we could sample the holes!*

"Please bring in two more buckets of water from the rain barrel," Mama instructed as she took out the last dough-nuts and slid the hot pan to the back of the stove. Opening the stovetop warmer, she checked the loaves of rising bread. "They're rising," she said. "But they're not quite ready to bake yet." She spoke mostly to herself. "I think I have time to take care of that lard in the oven first."

After filling both water pails from the barrel, I walked carefully across the porch so no water sloshed out. I set them down to open the screen door to the kitchen and saw Mama placing two tin pails close to the edge of the stove. I carried the water buckets into the room and set them on the floor behind Mama. *I'll wait to fill the reservoir until Mama is finished with the lard,* I thought.

"What are you doing, Mama?" Dora asked as she came into the kitchen.

"I need to put the melted lard from the oven into these pails," she said. "Please stay back. I don't want any hot lard to splash on you." Taking two thick hot pads, she opened the oven door. The smell of hot lard overpowered any lingering doughnut smell.

"It stinks!" Dora pinched her nose and left the kitchen.

I grabbed the broom from behind the door and went outside to sweep the porch. Mud clods dotted the floorboards, showing exactly where the men had walked that morning. *We sure don't need extra dirt slipping indoors! We have enough the way it is!* Marching toward the far end of the porch, I began to sweep.

Piercing screams suddenly rent the air. I jumped. *That's Mama screaming! What's wrong?* My heart began to pound. *Crash!*

Another agonizing scream sent me racing across the porch and into the house.

8

Courage to Go On

Throwing open the screen door, I saw smoking lard pooled around the stove and dripping from the overturned pan lying on the open oven door. Like hot lava flowing down a mountainside, the lard was creeping across the floor. Then I saw Mama. She was standing in the water pails I had just carried in—one foot in each bucket.

"Don't—step—in—the—lard," she gasped between moans. Her face was as white as a sheet. She hung onto the pantry door as if trying to hold herself up. *At least she's not screaming anymore,* I comforted myself.

The door at the other side of the room flew open, and I

sagged in relief to see Papa. *He will know what to do!*

"Marie!" Papa's frantic cry sent shock waves through me. Before I could blink, he was beside Mama, lifting her out of the buckets and carrying her to a kitchen chair. He set her on it and began removing her shoes.

"Oh-h, oh-h, oh-h," Mama kept moaning. Her eyes were shut, and her mouth was barely open. Her head was tilted at an odd, rigid angle, and her hands were clenched into tight fists.

I suddenly became aware of Mary's crying. I had forgotten everything but Mama. Quickly I picked up my baby sister, cuddling her close, wishing I could wake up and find this was just a bad dream. My chest hurt, and my heart was beating so hard I could feel my ribs moving.

Mama! I wanted to cry out. *Mama, are you going to be all right?* Instead, my thoughts became a prayer to God. *Dear Jesus, please take care of Mama.* I began trembling as Mama gave a gasp and fell back against the chair. Papa was pulling off her wet cotton stockings. I stared in horror to see large, thick pieces of skin clinging to them.

Pulling Mary close, I smothered my face against her hair. Even when I shut my eyes, I could not erase the ghastly sight of Mama's feet—raw and red, with skin peeling off.

I felt weak all over, but I knew I had to be brave for the younger children. What could I do? Dora was sobbing into my skirt; she had probably seen Mama's feet too. I put my free arm around her, trying to comfort her. Finally I looked up to see how Mama was doing. Papa was carrying her to the bedroom, his face lined with worry. I hugged Mary so hard she whimpered.

"Oh-h! Oh-h! Bern—Bern—" Mama's hushed, anguished cries paralyzed me.

Papa soon came back out of the bedroom. "Anna," he instructed, "tell Charles to go see if Mrs. Fraser can come. Mama needs her right away. He should tell her this is an emergency." Papa's tense instructions came as a relief. I did not feel so helpless if I had something to do. Mrs. Fraser was a neighbor lady who often helped people who were sick or injured.

Grabbing Dora's hand, I ran as fast as I could with Mary clinging to my neck. I splashed through puddles as I raced for the barn.

"Charles! Charles!" I hollered. "Where are you?"

Charles peered out of a calf pen, with Paul right beside him. "Why all the ruckus?" he asked.

"Mama's hurt bad!" I gasped. "Papa wants you to go get Mrs. Fraser. See if she can come right away! Tell her—tell her—Mama's feet are burned terribly from hot lard. Hurry!"

Charles must have been scared, because in one big leap he cleared the gate and raced out of the barn.

I didn't want to return to the house. I didn't want to hear Mama's moans. Her pain was more than I could imagine. I knew one small burn could hurt fiercely. *But both feet?* I shuddered and closed my eyes.

Suddenly I remembered the spilled lard. *Who will clean it up?* My heart sank. It was up to me. Everything Mama always did would fall on me until she was better. Everything! I shuddered again. It looked too big. *I can never do everything Mama did. Never.*

"Dora and Paul," I stopped and took a deep breath to steady my voice, "do you think you can play out here with Mary?" I knelt beside the calf pen to tell Paul what had happened. He peered at me through the pen boards, his mouth quivering, his eyes round with fright.

"Mama spilled hot lard on her feet," I explained. "The lard burned her feet really bad. You know how much a burn hurts, don't you?" He nodded. "Well, Mama's feet really hurt right now. We want to help her—don't we?" I turned to Dora. "I need both of you to help as much as you can."

"We will. Won't we, Paul?" Dora whispered. Paul nodded in agreement.

"Good! I knew you would!" My smile seemed to put them at ease. Then I continued, "You two stay out here and keep Mary happy. I'll go in and clean up the spilled lard. But as soon as I finish, I'll come back out to the barn. Okay?"

"Sure!" Paul brightened. "That will be fun! I like playing out here!"

"I can hold Mary on my lap, and we can slide down the hay pile." Dora reached for Mary, eager to help. "Or should we play church with Mary?"

"Church might be better," I said. "Mary is too little to slide down the hay, but we want to keep her happy." I gave them another bright smile, relieved when they began to set up to play church.

My chest hurt again. I knew I could count on them to be careful with Mary, but I dreaded facing what lay ahead.

"Dear Jesus," I cried as I stopped beside the barn door, leaning my head against its frame, "please help Mrs. Fraser be at home so she can come and help." I stayed a few more seconds, not even praying, but I felt a little better when I thought of God listening. *I'm sure Papa is praying, and Charles probably prayed the whole time he was running to the neighbors.* The thoughts brought comfort.

"And Mama is probably praying too!" I said aloud. "She prays about everything! I'm sure she is praying even if she hurts really bad. I know she is!"

With a lighter heart, I headed to the house.

Rain was still falling. As the raindrops splashed against me, I looked up at the clouds. Was heaven raining tears? Just the other Sunday when Brother James was preaching, he had said that angels rejoice when a sinner repents.

"If angels can rejoice, surely they can be sad too. I'm going to pretend they are crying with us." Saying my thoughts aloud helped me feel better. It gave me courage to open the screen door and enter the house. Before I had closed the door, Papa emerged from the bedroom. Deep lines still creased his face. "Where are the younger children?" he asked.

"Dora and Paul are keeping Mary in the barn." A lump lodged in my throat, and I could hardly say the words. Papa nodded as I whispered, "How is Mama?"

"Suffering. I'd like to get the doctor, but Mama says it wouldn't help. I'm not sure. I don't know much about burns." Papa sounded old and tired. He ran his hand through his thick, wavy hair, making it stand up. He did that when something bothered him or if he was trying to solve a problem.

No doctor? Does Mama really think the doctor can't help? Or is she afraid it would cost too much? Mama was always careful about spending money. *What if Mrs. Fraser can't help? What will we do then?*

I was afraid. I looked up at Papa and saw his worry. In a quiet voice I said, "I'm going to clean up the lard." He nodded and went back to the bedroom while I looked for something to scoop up the lard. All I could find was the metal turner we used to flip eggs or pancakes. The oven was still too hot to touch, but I could scrape off the puddles of lard by pushing them to the side of the door and letting them run into a pail beneath.

Mama is usually so careful…I wonder how the pan fell? It was even more puzzling when I remembered hearing her scream before I heard the crash. *What had happened? Why didn't Mama jump away? Why did God let this awful thing happen?* My questions and Mama's low moans coming from the bedroom frightened and confused me.

My foot bumped into a water pail and I gasped to see hardened white lard floating in the water. Lard from Mama's feet! My hand stopped as I stared at the water pails. *I'm sure glad I set them there.* Goosebumps peppered my arms. *Had this water helped Mama's feet? Did God make me put them there because He knew she would need them?*

The thought comforted me. I was almost done cleaning up the stove when a horse and buggy drove in. Looking out the window, my shoulders sagged in relief. It was Mrs. Fraser. God was sending help!

Papa was just as glad to see her. He quickly led her to the bedroom where Mama lay on the bed. *Thank you, God,* I breathed.

Once I had the oven door cleaned, I shut it and tackled the floor puddles. They were beginning to harden, making them easier to scoop up. I put the lard from the floor into a separate pail. I figured Mama would use it when she made soap after fall butchering. Once the floor lard was scraped up to the best of my ability, I filled a bucket with hot water and began washing the floor. I opened the reservoir lid to dip out more hot water and drew out only half a bucketful before I scraped the bottom. It was time to refill the reservoir.

Oh, no, I groaned as I reached for the water pails. *I'll have to wash these before I can get water!* There was nothing else to do but use my clean bucket of water to wash the water pails.

As I filled the two water pails at the barrel outside, I realized the rain had stopped. Only occasional drips fell from the roof. I could hear laughter in the barn and knew the younger ones were fine. Charles was back now. He would keep an eye on them.

It took both pails to fill the reservoir. Then I went back out and refilled the pails. Now I would have water waiting inside. When I put the lid back on the reservoir, I remembered the six loaves of bread in the warming oven.

The bread had risen so high it was falling over the sides of the pans. My heart sank. Too many things were happening. The stove was not hot enough, the bread dough had over-risen, Mama lay in bed badly hurt, and it was almost time for dinner.

I'll have to make dinner! I put my head in my hands. *What am I supposed to do?*

Immediately I straightened my drooping shoulders. I would stir up the fire. Mama always quoted, "When tasks are many, do the most important one first." That's what I would do.

There were enough hot coals in the firebox, so it didn't take long for the pine wood to catch fire. The merry crackling made me feel better. *I guess I'll just bake the bread and hope it doesn't fall,* I decided. *I'll get the skillet hot and fry one loaf for dinner. Bread and milk and a couple of doughnuts each will have to be enough.* "Besides," I muttered to myself, "I don't think I can eat. My stomach hurts."

I tested the reservoir water. Good—it was heating! I checked the oven gauge. *Still not quite 300 degrees. It has to be hotter than that!* "I'll just put the bread in anyway," I muttered. Quickly I opened the oven door, slid in five loaves, and shut the door.

What will we eat if it falls flat? I wondered. *Dear Jesus,* I prayed, *could you please help this bread bake right?*

By this time the water was hot enough when I dipped in my finger to test it. I filled my cleaning bucket and started scrubbing the floor around the stove with my soapy rag. As soon as I rinsed it out in the water, all the soap seemed to leave. I kept wiping up the grease and rinsing out my rag, washing as much of the floor as I could reach from one spot before moving on to the next area. *I might as well wash up all the grease before getting clean water.*

I could hear the low voices of Mrs. Fraser and Papa as they took care of Mama in the bedroom. When I went outside to empty my greasy water, I saw the sun trying to peep through the clouds. Birds were chirping and taking baths in the barnyard puddles. They didn't have a care in

Anna's Courage

the world! Several robins were searching for worms in the waterlogged grass.

I watched as one sang from the low branch that held our swing. Its song calmed me. *"Cheer up! Mama will get better!"* it seemed to say. I listened a few seconds longer before returning to my job. If the floor was to get cleaned before dinnertime, it was up to me!

When the floor was clean, I shut the stove damper and peeked at the bread. The loaves sagged in the middle and hung over the pans, but it wasn't flat like I had feared.

Two jobs done! I ticked them off in my mind—floor cleaning and bread baking. Time to fry! Taking the loaf of unbaked bread to the table, I pinched off small balls of dough. Flattening a few with my hands, I stretched out the spongy dough. I dropped one of them into the lard, but it sputtered only feebly. I busied myself stretching out the rest of the dough balls.

The next time I dropped in some dough, it sizzled more vigorously, singing out, *Just right! Just right! Fry more! Fry more!* A smile crept across my face as I dropped another flat piece of dough into the lard. It immediately started to bubble and puff up.

Suddenly I thought of the bread. *Taking care of everything is so hard! How can I fry dough and check the bread at the same time? I have only two hands and both are busy!* I wanted to run outside and leave all the work behind. But instead, I lifted out the piece of golden fried dough and added another one. I glanced at the table. *Seven more pieces to fry.*

When I took out the bread, it was dark, not a nice brown like Mama's, but I was relieved that it looked edible. *God has answered my prayer.* I closed the oven damper and viewed our meager dinner. My stomach growled. *The fried bread will not be enough! I could eat three pieces myself! Surely there is something in the pantry.* My mind ran in circles as I tried to think of something else I could prepare quickly. I checked the crock where Mama kept her cooked potatoes.

I gazed at the five little potatoes at the bottom of the crock. *Not enough.* Then I remembered Mama adding bread to stretch potatoes. *That's what I will do!* I carried the potatoes and a few slices of old bread to the table. Quickly I cubed the bread and sliced the potatoes, then I went to see if the skillet was still hot. I groaned. I had forgotten to check the fire!

And the wood box needs filled! Only one lonely chunk of firewood was still in the box. I gathered every small piece of bark and wood I could scrounge from the bottom of the box.

Suddenly Mrs. Fraser stepped into the kitchen. I glanced up at her and saw her looking at the loaves of bread, the plate of fried bread, and the heap of cold bread and potato slices. She came over to the stove where the skillet was heating.

"You can put your potatoes in. The lard is hot enough," she instructed quietly.

With shaking limbs, I did as she said. *What is she thinking? Is she going to scold me?* I cringed at the dark, misshapen loaves of bread glaring at us from the table.

"You're a brave girl," Mrs. Fraser said. Her gentle touch on my arm offered comfort as she continued, "Your mama will be able to rest better with your taking over. You have courage just like your mama. She is a brave, brave woman. I put a soda paste over her burns and bandaged them. Keeping the air off them should help a little with the pain. I'll be back this evening to check on her." She patted my arm and went out the door.

I sank onto the bench along the table and dropped my head into my hands. *She thinks I'm brave? And I have courage? If only she knew how scared I am!* I held back my tears. I didn't want Mama to know I was crying. How could I cry when she was being brave?

I felt all mixed up inside. I wanted to see Mama, to talk to her, but I was scared to go into the bedroom. *How will she look? Will she see I am afraid?* I turned the potatoes over, then got the dishrag and wiped both my tears and the table. As I set the table for dinner, Papa came out of the bedroom.

"Come, Anna," he said, beckoning with his hand. "Mama wants you." His smile gave me courage. I set down the last plate and followed him. *Be brave, be brave,* I told myself. But the nearer I came to the doorway, the faster and harder my heart thumped. Papa must have read my expression, for he laid his hand on my shoulder and whispered, "It will be okay, Anna." His words were a balm to my troubled heart. I gathered myself together and pushed back the tears ready to spill. Quietly I entered the room.

Mama lay on the bed, her bandaged feet propped on a rolled-up blanket. Her face was white, and her forehead was wet with beads of sweat. She opened her eyes and tried to smile, but suddenly she trembled. Her lips became a thin line, and her eyes closed again as a wave of pain passed through her. As quickly as it had come, it was gone. Mama took a shallow breath and opened her eyes. I was immediately at her side.

"Mama," I choked, "I cleaned up the lard and baked the bread. It rose too much, but we can still eat it. I fried a loaf for dinner and made the last of the potatoes." My words rushed together as tears ran down my face, but I wanted Mama to know things were getting done. "You can rest, Mama. I'll do the work and take care of the children. They are with Charles in the barn right now."

"I—know—I can—depend—on you." Mama's breathing was labored, and she fought to keep her eyes open. I could see the pain returning. I wanted to do something, but there

Anna's Courage

was nothing I could do. "Pray," she whispered and reached out to touch me.

"I will," I answered and stumbled out of the bedroom. I could hardly bear to see her suffering. "Papa, I'll get the children in. Dinner is ready." I forced the words through the heavy blanket of fear that was trying to smother me. I clung to Mama's words: *I know I can depend on you. Pray.* I repeated them over and over in my mind.

As I walked to the barn, I began praying. "Dear Jesus, I don't know how I can take care of things!" I took a deep breath. "I need you to help me, Jesus. It looks too big for me." I wiped my eyes on my dress sleeve. "Dear Jesus, I don't want Mama to worry. I want her to get better. Please, Jesus, could you touch her and heal her? Like the woman in the Bible? If it is your will? In Jesus' name. Amen."

I looked up into the clouds and thought about the familiar Bible story. All the sick woman did was touch the hem of Jesus' robe and she was made well. What if Jesus would reach down and heal Mama like that? What if I found her walking around when I got back to the house?

"Oh, I wish that would happen," I whispered.

I remembered a recent discussion during our morning worship. Dora had asked why she had never seen anyone being healed. "Dora," Papa had explained, "when Jesus was on earth, many people lived in darkness. They did not have the Bible or the Holy Spirit living in their hearts. They did not have churches preaching the truth. Those people needed to see miracles so they would listen to Jesus' words and believe in Him."

I sighed. I still wished God would send an angel or miraculously heal Mama.

Mama wanted me to pray for her. But I knew she also wanted me to ask God for my own strength. *I'm only eleven!* I wanted to protest. *How can I possibly do everything she usually does?*

Once again I could hear Mama saying, "When tasks are many, do the most important one first."

I squared my shoulders. As I had been doing all morning, I would try to figure out the most important job and do that one first.

9

Doing the Next Thing

By the time the supper dishes were finished, I was so tired I thought I couldn't do one more thing. *Does Mama ever feel like this?* I wondered. Wearily I dipped water out of the reservoir for the girls' baths. Papa had offered to make pancakes for dinner tomorrow. He had no idea how much that meant to me. It was as if a great burden had rolled off my shoulders. I did not have to think of food for tomorrow! What a blessing.

Sunday morning dawned with a hint of frost. As I threw out the dirty dishwater, the stiff wind reminded me that winter was not far away. I looked at the empty garden, thankful we had dug our potatoes. As Mama often said, "Add it to your thankful list. There is always something to be thankful for!"

Mrs. Fraser came that morning and changed Mama's bandages. "I have a surprise," Papa told us after she had left. He disappeared into the bedroom while we waited expectantly. "Come," he beckoned. "If you all stand quietly by the wall, we will have a short service with Mama."

Mama's face was pinched and pale, and it took her a moment before she could smile at us. I suspected she was fighting pain. Mary immediately reached for her, and Papa gently set her on the bed near Mama's arm.

"Come, dear," Mama murmured, and Mary lay down beside her, content to have Mama close. She was only fifteen months old, but she seemed to understand that Mama was hurt.

"Let's pray," Papa instructed. We bowed our heads as Papa prayed. "Our kind, wise, and all-knowing heavenly Father, we come to you this morning, thanking you for your care and protection. We ask for your healing hand on Mama. Lord God, bless her with strength. If it is not against your will, we pray for relief from the pain. Give us wisdom to know what to do for her burns.

"Bless each of the children as we work together in the coming weeks. Help each of us to serve you faithfully and to live obedient lives that bear fruit. May your will be done. Amen."

"Please sing 'Little Children, Praise the Lord,'" Mama suggested softly.

"Children," Papa said when the song was finished, "are you questioning why God allowed this accident to happen?"

"I wish it hadn't," Dora sniffed. Her lips trembled, and she tried not to cry.

"Come." Mama patted the bed. Dora needed no second invitation. She made a beeline for the bed, with Paul following right behind.

"Yes, Dora," Papa sympathized. "We all wish it had not happened. But it did, and we are thankful it was not worse."

"How could it be worse?" Charles asked, his brow creased with doubt. "Burns are terrible!"

"I agree," Papa replied. "And Mama's burns are causing her a lot of pain. But something prevented them from being even worse."

"The water buckets?" I asked.

"Yes, the buckets of cold water."

"Mama, what really happened?" I blurted out.

"I was taking the lard out of the oven," Mama explained. "I had let it cool down a little because I knew the big pan would be heavy. Hot lard is dangerous, so I used heavy hot pads to protect my hands. I didn't want to burn my hands if some lard splashed up as I poured it into the pails. I lifted the pan very carefully out of the oven and was ready to tip it into the waiting pail when the pan tipped backward, spilling lard onto my feet.

"I could hardly bear the searing pain. Those two water pails were right beside me, and all I could think of was that water stops heat. I must have dropped the pan before I stepped into the pails. I don't remember." Her voice had grown quiet, and we had to strain to hear her.

"The water did help," Papa said. "And wearing shoes also helped."

"Was it God who had me set the water pails right beside the stove?" I asked. "If Mama is working at the stove, I usually set the buckets just inside the door, but this time I carried them over close to the stove. I don't know why I did that."

"I'm sure God gives us nudges to do things we don't normally do," Papa assured me. "Because you put the buckets there, Mama had water right beside her when she needed it. But maybe you wonder why God didn't make the lard spill away from Mama. I have wondered the same thing," Papa confessed.

"But we don't need to know why. We just need to remember that even though God allowed the accident to happen, He loves us and cares for us. We need to accept this as something God wants our family to go through. And we want to keep trusting Him no matter what He sends.

"*Courage* is the word I want to talk about this morning. It will be our Sunday school lesson for today. What does God tell us about courage? 1 Chronicles 28:20 will be today's memory verse: 'Be strong and of good courage, and do it: fear not, nor be dismayed: for the Lord God, even my God, will be with thee; he will not fail thee, nor forsake thee.'

"King David spoke these words to his son Solomon when he was giving him instructions for building the temple. It must have seemed like an impossible task to Solomon. The Bible tells us that Solomon was young, and the work was great. King David wanted his son to realize that God would be with him. All he needed was courage to do the next thing. Solomon was to begin the work and keep at it until it was done."

"I need that verse as much as Solomon," Mama said.

I was shocked. *Mama needs courage? Why, Mama always has courage! She is always smiling, singing, laughing, telling stories, and making work interesting. Maybe she means courage to endure her burns.*

"Be strong and of good courage." I repeated the words aloud to myself as we left the bedroom. *I'm going to copy that verse on a piece of paper and tack it up in the kitchen. That way I can read it and remember it. Mrs. Fraser said I was brave—but*

I don't think I am. I think she knew I would need courage to do what needs to be done.

"Papa, what is courage?" I heard Charles ask from the living room where he and Papa were sitting.

"That is a good question, son. Let me try to explain. Courage can be something we do or something we think. God told Solomon to have courage and build. It would take determination to build the temple. It would take strength and perseverance to complete the work. So courage can mean doing something when we are afraid, or it might be tackling something hard or new for us.

"Suppose I was hurt instead of Mama. Let's say I broke my leg and was lying in bed. I couldn't walk or drive the horses. Rain is coming, and a wagonload of hay is sitting out in the field. Suppose you had never hitched up a team alone, and no one is here to help you. How would you feel?"

"I suppose I would be scared," Charles said. "I'm not sure I could do it."

I leaned against the kitchen table to listen. I didn't want to miss a word.

"Yes," Papa agreed. "I'm sure you would feel scared. But remember, it looks dark out and we are going to get a heavy rain. If you don't get the hay in, the whole load will be ruined. You hear thunder in the distance."

Charles shivered at the picture Papa was painting. "I

suppose I would run out to the barn and get the horses. But I think I would pray first. Then I would try to harness them and head for the field."

Papa smiled. "That is one example of courage—doing the right thing even if it seems hard." He put his hand on Charles's shoulder. "Courage can also be the strength to *not* do something. To refuse to yield to sin or to fight back when someone mistreats us.

"And sometimes courage is just cheerfully accepting something we cannot change. Think about Mama. She needs courage to endure the pain and courage to be patient. Don't you think it's hard for her to lie in bed and not be able to help with the work?"

Charles nodded. I imagined he was thinking the same thing I was. *Mama is always busy taking care of us. How hard it must be for her to stay in bed and do nothing!*

"Remember, son, God never asks us to do something we cannot do. Courage is being brave when we are in difficulty. It is asking God for strength to do what is right, no matter what. It is doing the work God asks us to do. Having courage means accepting things instead of complaining."

I surely needed to hear that! I rubbed my forehead, deep in thought. *Can I really do that?*

That afternoon Mrs. Fraser came again to change Mama's bandages. "I was told raw potatoes will help draw out the heat, Marie. Shall we try some?" she asked.

Mama did not hesitate. "I've never heard of that, but I'm willing to try it."

Charles brought potatoes up from the cellar while I drew water to wash and peel them. Knowing Mama's pain was intense, I grated them as quickly as I could. It was a messy job, sending splatters in all directions, but I didn't care. *Please, God, let these help,* I prayed as I peeled and grated.

I watched Mama closely as Mrs. Fraser took a handful of shredded potatoes and gently laid them on her feet. Mama jerked. Her eyes widened and she took a deep breath, but almost instantly she relaxed. "The cool dampness feels good. I believe this might help."

After Mrs. Fraser left, Mary sat beside Mama. "Shine, shine, just where you are," she lisped. "Shine, shine, just where you are." Over and over she sang the short phrase of the song, and its sweet message went straight to my heart. *I will try to do that,* I decided.

"Uncle David's family is here!" Paul shouted as he dashed inside—then back out to meet the horse and buggy pulling up to the hitching post.

"Our cousins!" I cried, grabbing the dishrag to wipe up the potato mess from the table.

"Irene is here!" Dora clapped her hands and ran out the door.

Suddenly I felt light and free, and the rest of the day stretched delightfully ahead. I hadn't realized I was carrying such a burden until it lifted. *Aunt Mary is here! I don't have to worry about one more thing! She probably brought our supper and a good many other things.* My mind spun wildly.

I ran out to the buggy, calling, "Do you know Mama got burned? I'm so glad you came!" As the words spilled out, I couldn't stop the rush of pent-up emotions. With a sob, I fell into Aunt Mary's arms.

"We came as soon as we could. I couldn't stay away." Aunt Mary held me as I cried, her comfort a soothing balm to my heart.

Many decisions were made for Mama's care before Uncle David and Aunt Mary left. Mrs. Fraser had passed the news of the accident on to her neighbors, and they in turn had kept the message going. Many kind people offered to help. Two ladies would come every Tuesday to help with the wash. Others would send food. The neighbor boys would come to milk the cows so Papa could concentrate on harvest. Even our new schoolteacher, Mr. Olson, had volunteered to help with the milking several times a week.

"Anna," Papa said after he had explained the work plan to me at Mama's bedside that evening, "it will be weeks until

Mama can get up and walk. You will need to stay home from school to care for the little ones. Mr. Olson said he will bring your lessons on the days he milks the cows and will explain any new work."

I was stunned. *I'll have to miss school? Why, it has just started!* My heart sank and my throat choked up. I looked at Mama lying in bed with her bandaged feet, then I glanced at Papa. He had barely started with the harvest, and there would be weeks of fieldwork. Maybe as many weeks as it would take Mama to get better. My heart sank even lower.

I can't miss school! I wanted to wail. *I don't want to stay at home for weeks on end!*

But I didn't let my troubled thoughts tumble out. I held them in so tightly it felt like a rope was squeezing me tighter and tighter with each breath. My heart pounded. I wanted to run outside. I wanted to run to the barn and cry instead of trying to be brave.

Suddenly Mary's sweet lisping song came to my memory. *Shine, shine, just where you are. Shine, shine, just where you are.* The words rang over and over in my mind.

Courage. I swallowed the lump in my throat. *Courage.* The pounding in my heart slowed down. *Courage.* The tightness around my chest began to ease. *Courage.* I would try to be strong and of good courage.

"You won't have to do everything, Anna," Mama said.

"Only the most important things matter right now. But thanks for your willingness. I don't know what we would do without you. I'll have Dora and Paul help you all they can." Mama's voice sounded weak. She looked exhausted, and her face was still pale. Dark circles ringed her eyes, and when she wiped the sweat from her forehead, her hand was trembling.

"I don't mind staying at home," I blurted out. "I don't mind at all!" It hurt me to see Mama hurting. All I wanted was for her to get better as fast as she could.

I left the bedroom and went to wash up Mary for bedtime. "Your feet are green!" I said, tickling her toes as I scrubbed off the evidence of a happy evening outdoors. She giggled. I smiled as I thought of the fun time we had enjoyed with our cousins. Choosing teams and playing "Andy Over" with an old sock holding a rag-covered rock had been great fun! Whenever we suspected the other side had caught the sock, we would sweep up the little ones in our arms or give them piggyback rides as we raced around our old woodshed. I laughed aloud as I remembered Charles being the lone player on his side and how he had outsmarted us by waiting so long. We had come bursting around the corner, thinking all was clear, when he popped out right in our faces! He had tagged us all in one sweep—Edith and I, Dora and Irene, and the little ones we were hauling along!

Mary laughed with me. It was with a lighter heart that I tucked her into bed. Blowing out the lamp, I knelt beside my bed to pray.

Mama continued to suffer searing waves of pain—pain that had hardly lessened since the accident the day before. None of us knew until months later how nearly Mama had passed out when the hot lard burned her feet. No one knew how often she cried out to God for strength to hang on to her senses.

Though the pain was almost more than she could handle, God heard her prayers and gave her strength and courage.

10

Creaking Stairs and Crumbly Bread

Mama had me put grated potatoes on her feet in the morning, afternoon, and evening on Monday. "I think they look a little better," I told her that evening.

"The pain is not as sharp," she acknowledged. *Sharp? What does Mama mean?* Sharp pain was really bad pain. I could not imagine what "not as sharp" meant. I shuddered inwardly and tenderly applied the potatoes.

On Tuesday morning Mrs. Fraser clucked her tongue against the roof of her mouth to show her pleasure. "I'm highly pleased with your feet. I see no signs of infection. It's barely three days since your accident, but I think we can start using Rawleigh's salve. The salve will help prevent infection and scabbing. We sure don't want to remove any scabs. That would be very painful."

I watched her spread a liberal layer of brown salve over the burns. Even though Mrs. Fraser was as gentle as possible, I saw Mama gripping the bed so hard her knuckles looked like they would burst through her skin. I had to leave. I went to check the stove's firebox and added more wood. The ladies coming to do the wash would soon be here, and I wanted to be ready.

It wasn't until I heard Mama say, "Thank you, that feels better," that I returned to the bedroom where she half lay, half sat against the pillows. Her bandaged feet were propped on a rolled-up blanket and her hands were resting on her lap. I always looked at her hands; they would tell me if she was having bad pain.

"Those potatoes did the trick, Anna," Mrs. Fraser said quietly. "But now that we are using salve, we won't need to use them anymore."

By the time Mrs. Fraser left, I had gathered the wash. Under Mama's watchful eye, I separated the items into piles and placed the stained clothes to soak in a tub of soapy water. Papa and Charles had filled the washing machine and rinse tubs with water before the children left for school. All was ready when the wash ladies arrived.

I was looking forward to the day. Mama had reminded me last evening that I would not have to fix food on wash day. "I'm glad for your sake that the ladies are bringing both dinner and supper tomorrow."

What will they bring? I wondered for what seemed the hundredth time. *I hope not fried potatoes and canned pork chunks!* That was about all we had been eating, and probably would for the next six weeks. Fixing meals three times a day was hard work! I had never dreamed it would take so much time. *Surely we will have something different today!*

My work done for once, I raced out the kitchen door. Grabbing the swing, I stood on the wooden seat and started pumping. Papa said it was Indian summer, and I hoped it would last for weeks and weeks. At least until Papa finished the harvest. My thoughts took flight until I saw a buggy coming down the road. Dragging one foot, I slowed the swing, jumped off, and headed for the house.

Yum! Chicken and dumplings! My mouth watered as I set the table for dinner a few hours later. I couldn't wait to dig in. Rich gravy bubbled up between plump dumplings, covering a thick chicken stew beneath. A gallon jar of cooked apples with cinnamon waited on the sideboard. *Hooray! No canned meat or fried potatoes today!*

The next days passed in a blur of never-ending work. Each day Mama's pain lessened and applying the salve became a little easier. But by the time Saturday arrived, I woke up feeling tired and grumpy. The floors were dirty, the lamps needed to be washed, and bread needed to be baked. Everyone was home from school, and I would have to make breakfast, dinner, and supper for all of them. Hair had to be washed and the beds stripped and remade. The list seemed to go on and on and on.

I pulled myself out of bed, jerked on my dress, and went to wake Dora and Paul. "Hurry! Get up and get dressed," I snapped. "If Mary wakes up, bring her down."

I wanted to go back to bed and let Mama take care of everything. But no, it was up to me. I needed to start the porridge for breakfast and do a hundred other jobs.

Yesterday I had scorched the porridge. We still ate it because it was all we had for breakfast. But what an awful way to start the day. And today wasn't starting off much better.

This is too hard! Tears threatened, and a knot tightened in the middle of my chest. It grew heavier with each step. "I just can't do everything," I moaned, and the steps answered, *Cour-age.* At least that is what the *creak-creak* sounded like. I listened as I took another step down. *Cour-age,* the step creaked.

Courage? I had forgotten all about courage. Down, down the stairs I went, listening for each creak of courage. I wondered about Mama. Did she need courage to stay in bed day after day? Mrs. Fraser had said I was brave like Mama. I straightened my shoulders; I did not want to disappoint Mama. I would try to have courage today. The lump in my chest began to leave. I blinked away the tears and took a firm step down. *Cour-age!* The step creaked extra boldly, and a tiny smile tugged at the corners of my mouth.

I thought of Psalm 27:14, a verse we were memorizing: "Wait on the Lord; be of good courage. Wait on the Lord; be of good courage. Wait on the Lord; be of good courage." Each time I said it, I felt more ready to begin the morning work. "Wait on the Lord…" I reached the bottom of the stairs and stopped. I couldn't believe my eyes!

"Mama, are you better?" I asked. I was shocked to see her sitting in her rocking chair. Her feet were propped up on the footstool. It seemed almost like normal!

"Good morning, Anna," she answered with a smile. "My feet are healing, and I'm thankful to be out of the bedroom."

"But how did you get out here? Can you walk?"

"Papa carried me. Lord willing, I plan to join all of you as much as possible and help with the work if I can."

"Oh, Mama! I'm so glad!" This was an unexpected surprise. *Mama is getting better! She will be directing the work, not me!* My heart felt light and free.

What a difference it made to have Mama sitting in the

kitchen! She sat close to the wide archway to the living room and could see the activity in both rooms. Instead of clinging to me, Mary was free to climb up and sit on Mama's lap. Paul and Dora joined her when they could, making good use of the rocking chair's two wide, sturdy arms. Work was no longer drudgery. Mama's presence was like a cup of joy spilling into everything I did.

"Bring me the potatoes in a bowl and I will peel them,"

Anna's Courage

she said. She did not sit idle. If she wasn't holding Mary, her hands were busy with the mending pile or doing some other task. That evening I went to bed without dreading the next day. Papa had said he would carry Mama out each morning until she could walk.

It was Tuesday again. I woke up earlier than usual. The kitchen door closed with a bang as Papa left the house. I pulled the covers over my head to block out the morning sunlight until I suddenly remembered what day it was— wash day! Quickly I tossed back the covers and jumped out of bed. Two church ladies would be coming again to help. I couldn't wait to see who came, and what all we could get accomplished. *I'd better get to work,* I told myself. *There's still a lot to do before they arrive.*

"Mama, this is the last loaf of bread," I said as I cut slices for breakfast and school lunches.

"We will bake bread today," she replied.

"Good!" I said. "I'm tired of cutting these funny loaves and eating crumbly bread." I chuckled as I held up the lop-sided, dark-looking bread.

"Just be thankful we could eat it," came her quiet reprimand.

My laughter died when I thought of Mama's accident

and the reason the bread looked like it did. It was hard to believe it was now ten days since it had happened. "Do you think God kept the bread from falling flat?" I asked. I brushed the remaining crumbs from the table into my hand and popped them into my mouth. "The bread had risen way too high, and the oven wasn't hot enough when I put it in."

"I believe He did." Mama smiled at me as she closed her Bible. "If you had put it into a hot oven, the change in temperature would have made the bread puff up even higher and then collapse. God took care of our need by having you put the bread into a cooler-than-normal oven."

I had not thought of God taking care of us in that way. First had been the buckets of water I had carried in. Then the cool oven that saved the bread from disaster. And all the help we had received since then. A sense of wonder filled me. *God did care about the smallest things! Even if God didn't save Mama from getting hurt, He is taking care of our needs, like Papa said.*

Charles and Dora had just left for school when our help arrived. Once more the women took over with the washing. They took turns working the handle back and forth on our hand-powered washing machine. Their steady rhythm kept the agitator going back and forth, cleaning the clothes.

I was overjoyed when the ladies suggested I work on my school lessons unless they needed me for something. I was behind in my schoolwork, and maybe now I could catch up with my class. Mr. Olson would bring my new lessons when he came to milk the cows on Thursday.

"I can't wait to surprise Mr. Olson!" I exclaimed. I beamed at Mama as I sat down at the table and began my lessons.

11

Mama's Stories

"Put the next batch of clothes on a chair beside me," Mama said when I dumped a load of clean laundry onto the table. The wash ladies had left, and I hoped I could bring in all the dry clothes before Charles and Dora arrived home from school.

A chicken was roasting in the oven for our supper, and a pan of creamy noodles with peas waited to be reheated. The cookie jar was full of molasses cookies, and six loaves of golden bread and two pans of cinnamon rolls cooled on the table. The women had even made three pies and a spice crumb cake! My mouth watered, and one of Mama's sayings came to mind: *Many hands make light work.*

That is surely true! I mused as I unpinned the dry sheets from the line. I breathed in the fresh smell of clean laundry and thought over the happy, busy day. *What would we do without our kind neighbors and church people? Maybe the weeks will go faster than I thought they would!*

"Hi!" I called out to Charles and Dora as they ran up the lane, swinging their lunch pails.

When I entered the house with the last armload of wash, I heard Dora begging. "Please, Mama, tell us a story while we fold clothes. This is such a big pile!" She glared at the pile of clothes, and I knew she must be tired from her day at school.

"Yes, a story would be fun," I agreed, dumping the last armload on top of the heaped-up chair.

"Give me a minute," Mama promised. "Anna, please bring another chair and put some of the clothes on that. It will be easier for me to reach."

"It looks like we have a whole mountain of clothes to fold!" I laughed. "Dora, you can help

Mama fold her pile. If it looks like you're going to beat me, I can always add more to your stack!"

"Tell the story about fetching the cows when Anna was little!" Dora said. I was glad to see her frown disappear as she giggled and sneaked a sly peek at me.

"You just want to hear that one because I was naughty, don't you?" I wrinkled my nose at her, pretending to be upset. Dora laughed, revealing the gap where a front tooth was missing. Picking up a washcloth, she snapped it at me before laying it on the table. I watched her smooth it neatly in half, making sure the corners touched evenly. *How like Dora!* I mused. *She is one particular little girl!*

Mama smiled and began the story. "Many summers ago, the only people who lived at our house were Papa, myself, and two sweet little children who were really babies. Anna was not quite two and Charles was almost five months old. One of my jobs while Papa was working in the fields was to bring in the cows and milk them before supper. I didn't mind doing the outdoor chores, but it was hard with two little children. What could I do with them while I brought in the cows? I couldn't carry both of them, and it was too far for Anna to walk."

"Was Charles a baby?" Paul questioned. His brow was puckered, and I could see he was having a hard time imagining that.

"Yes, he was. Smaller than Mary is now. You were once a little baby too, Paul. Even Papa and I were babies at one time!" Mama chuckled at his confusion and gave him a hug as he leaned over the arm of the rocking chair.

"Each time I had to bring in the cows, I tried to think of a way to leave the two children in the house. If all went well, I could have the cows inside the corral in about ten minutes. Charles was fine in his crib. But little Anna climbed everywhere she could! If I put her in the crib with Charles, she would climb over the side before I even got to the pasture!"

Dora giggled and Paul snickered. Both looked up at me, their eyes sparkling.

"That evening when it was time to do the chores, I still hadn't come up with any new ideas. So I put Charles in his crib with a toy—a stuffed, knitted cat. He loved chewing on its long tail or flopping it around."

"Like this!" Dora grabbed a sock and waved it in front of Mary's face, making her laugh—until the sock caught her across the eye and she started wailing.

"Dora, shall I stop the story? Are you working?" Mama's voice was stern.

Dora wilted. "I'm sorry, Mary." She kissed her sister's eye and wiped the tears. "Sorry, Mama. I'll get to work. Please keep telling the story."

"When I had Charles happy in his crib, I got a scarf to

tie Anna to a chair. I put the chair near the table, put Anna on it, and tied the scarf securely around her. Then I gave her a piece of bread to eat, hoping it would keep her occupied and out of mischief.

"'Anna,' I said, 'be a big girl and sit right here until Mama gets back. Mama needs to go outside and bring in the cows.' Little Anna took a bite of her jam bread and smacked her lips. She seemed happy, sitting quietly, so I hurried out the door.

"Walking swiftly down the pasture lane, I started calling, 'Come, boss. Come, boss,' hoping the cows would come when they heard me call. They often did that. They would raise their heads as if they had been listening for my call. Then they would start ambling toward home, with Bessie's cowbell ringing as she took the lead. But sometimes Bessie acted contrary and just kept right on grazing, paying no attention to my call. When that happened, I had to chase them in.

"I didn't have to call very long that day until Bessie lifted her head and came walking toward me. The two other cows followed behind her, one after the other, like they were playing follow the leader. Those cows used the same path to and from the pasture just like our cows do today.

"I was so glad the cows were coming in on their own. I kept thinking of Anna. Was she still tied to the chair? Was she still eating her bread or had she wriggled loose? I didn't like to leave my little children alone in the house, but I had no other choice. There was nothing else to do! Every time I went to bring in the cows, I prayed and asked Jesus to keep my babies out of danger.

"As soon as I had the cows in the corral, I hurried to the house. I could see through the kitchen window before I got there, and lo and behold, Anna was not in her chair! 'Oh my,' I thought, 'what is she doing?' I ran the last little distance and threw open the door. There sat Anna on the floor in the middle of a mess! Buttons, pins, and sewing needles were scattered all across the floor! She had somehow reached my sewing basket and dumped everything out. Charles lay on his tummy in his crib, watching Big Sister make a mess!"

Mama looked at the dwindling pile of unfolded clothes and said, "Anna, maybe you could sprinkle the clothes that need ironing while the younger ones and I finish folding them. Get a bowl of water, then I think I have time to tell another short story—one I don't think I have ever told before."

"Yes!" we all cried in unison.

"This is another cow story," Mama began. "It happened when Anna and Charles were about a year and a half older. This time the cows did not come when I called, so I had to walk all the way out to where they were grazing and chase them home. I was getting worried by the time I made it back to the house. What a sight met my eyes! Both Anna and Charles were sitting ON the kitchen table, surrounded by cups! My good water glasses were lined up on the window ledge, and the glass water pitcher sat at the very edge of the table!"

"What did you do?" Dora gasped.

"The first thing I did was grab the water pitcher and rescue the glasses. Then I lifted Anna and Charles off the table. Anna didn't say a word; she just looked at me with her big brown eyes." Mama made her eyes big and wide without a smile on her face.

Dora and Paul burst out laughing, and I had to laugh with them.

"I could tell Anna knew she had been naughty," Mama continued. "But I could not imagine how she had gotten the water glasses down from the cupboard without breaking any, or how she had placed the heavy pitcher up on the table!"

"How did she, Mama?" Dora asked.

"I don't know," Mama chuckled. "I wasn't there to see it!"

"And I don't know either!" I grinned. "I don't remember a thing!" Then I asked Mama a question that had occurred to me during the first story. "Did you take us to the barn when you milked the cows?"

"Yes, I did. When Charles was little, I would take two

milk pails to the barn. I would put Charles into one of them, and you hung onto the other one as we walked to the barn. Charles would grip the sides of the pail with his tight little fists and never make a peep. I think he felt safe inside the pail!

"It wasn't easy to milk while I minded two babies, but it helped that Charles was content to sit in the milk pail beside me, and you were happy to stand and watch the milk stream into the bucket.

"How different it is to do the chores today! Not only outdoor chores, but indoor chores like folding these clothes. Since you children are old enough to help, it makes the work so much easier!

"When Anna was little, I would finish milking the cows and then carry both Charles and a full bucket of milk to the house. I needed to strain the milk and pour it into the cream separator and crank the handle myself. Then I carried the skim milk out to the pigs and calves.

"What a blessing it is to have children old enough to help! Cheerful, dependable children. When I had to stay in bed last week, I did not worry that Mary would get into things. I knew you three were looking after her and keeping her happy. Dora, I knew you were being a big help to Anna, and Paul was doing his best. When it was mealtime, I heard dishes clatter as you set the table, and I could rest.

I heard you talking to each other as you washed dishes and swept the floor. I heard Paul playing nicely with Mary and heard Charles asking if there was anything else he could do to help.

"Thank you, children. I was blessed to hear you working together. I believe your cheerfulness helped me heal quicker.

"Now it is time to put the clothes away and set the table for supper. We don't want Papa and Charles to come in and find us sitting around telling stories instead of doing our work!" Mama chuckled.

It was wonderful to hear her laugh again.

12

A Special Gift

One day Mama noticed a hard, inflamed lump on her right foot. When Mrs. Fraser stopped in to see how she was doing, Mama asked her about it.

"It looks like proud flesh," Mrs. Fraser said. "I would try a brown sugar poultice. That works on horses when they have an injury, and I think it should help you. I'll make a paste of sugar and water and put it on for you before I leave. Anna can see how thick I make it—just enough water to hold the sugar together. She should change the poultice twice a day."

"I never heard of that remedy before, but it's worth a try." Mama was grateful for any help she could receive.

The sugar poultices did the trick. After several days, the ulcer-like red flesh began to go away. *Thank you, Jesus,* I prayed in my heart. After about a week, Mama's skin lay smooth against the top of her foot again.

Six long weeks had passed since the accident. Papa still carried Mama to and from the bedroom, as she was afraid to put any weight on her tender feet. Her feet still looked awful, but we were happy to see the ugly, purple-red blotches getting smaller. Thin new skin was growing over the burned areas.

"Bernhard," I heard her say one day as she sat in her chair, "I would like to try standing today."

I looked up in surprise. I could see surprise on Papa's face as well.

"Are you sure, Marie? We don't want to do anything too soon."

"Yes," Mama answered firmly. "After sitting for six weeks, I would like to try it. I won't walk, just stand for a little."

Papa seemed reluctant to move the footstool, but he did. "Anna, come stand on Mama's other side in case she starts to fall. I'm not too sure about this." He ran his hand through his hair, and worry lines crossed his forehead.

"I've been sitting so long, and the pain is almost gone," Mama urged.

I almost gasped out loud. *Mama still has pain? I didn't*

dream her burns still hurt! After six weeks!

"Look at how much they have healed." Mama raised her feet a little to show us.

Papa and I were the only ones in the kitchen as Mama gripped the rocker arms and pushed herself up. Papa suggested he and I help lift her under her arms so she would not have her full weight on her feet all at once. "Lift, Anna," he instructed as Mama started to stand.

I could feel Mama trembling beneath my hands when she suddenly cried out, "Put me down!"

We lowered her into the rocking chair, and I saw blood dripping from her right foot.

"It was too soon," she gasped. "I felt the pressure pop something." She lay back against the rocker and closed her eyes. Her face was white and beads of sweat dotted her forehead.

"You broke a blood vessel. I'm sorry, Marie. It was too much weight."

I felt like crying as I got a wet rag and wiped up the floor. *How much longer will it be until Mama is better? How much longer will I have to stay home from school?* For one brief instant I had let my hopes soar. Maybe I could soon go back to school. What fun it would be to see Shirley again! Now those hopes had burst. They were dripping away like the blood on Mama's foot.

I felt angry and frustrated. I was tired of staying home. Tired of having to work like a mama while Shirley and Cousin Edith went off to school. They could wake up in the morning and eat a breakfast they did not have to fix. Then after school they could come home to a hot supper cooking on the stove. They had help to clean the house, and they didn't have to bathe a little sister or wash another sister's hair.

I must have looked like a thundercloud, because Papa gave me a stern look as he gently placed Mama's feet back onto the footstool. I tried to clear my thoughts, but they kept tumbling around and around in my head. Suddenly I was too tired to think. Grabbing an empty water bucket, I fled from the house and let my tears fall as I pumped water from the pump. It took a long time to fill the bucket. No one called me, and I did not want to return to the house until I could face my parents without my feelings showing on my face.

Cour-age. Cour-age... the pump creaked.

Courage? Ha! I'm tired of that word! I gritted my

teeth. *I don't want courage! All I want is to go back to school!* My insides felt all mixed up. I wished it was bedtime so I could go to sleep and not have to do anything more today.

Dry leaves crunched under my feet as I shuffled across the yard. I looked up at the clouds drifting across the sky. A hawk glided to the top of the barn. Everything was free but me.

"Anna." The sharpness of Papa's voice startled me. I hadn't even noticed he was outside. I looked up at him, and the kindness I saw on his face made me burst into tears. "Anna," he said again, and this time his tone was gentle as he rested a hand on my shoulder. "Mama feels so bad. She is weary of sitting all day, making you work hard while she does so little. She hates being a burden, and she wants badly to be a mother again so you can go back to school."

"I'm sorry, Papa," I sobbed. "I don't know what is wrong with me. I want to help Mama—I truly do. But I feel all mixed up, and I don't know why."

Papa spoke softly. "I know you want to help—and we couldn't get along without you. But today we'd like to give you a break. Go wash your face and change your dress. I think you can make it to school by first recess. Mama will send a note to Mr. Olson. Take your books and enjoy the next few hours. I'm going to stay around the house and take care of Mama."

A Special Gift

"Really, Papa? I can go to school today?" I wanted to jump for joy. *I am going to be with my school friends!* "Thank you!" I finally squeaked out. Excitedly I ran for the house, forgetting all about the water. Papa picked up the bucket and followed me.

I raced into the house and ran to Mama. "Oh, Mama! Thank you! I can hardly wait! But are you sure you don't need me?" I stopped, some of my joy escaping when I saw her foot with the burst blood vessel. It was spread with brown salve. I was ashamed of the ugly feelings I had harbored when I left the house.

"I can stay," I whispered.

"No, Papa will do just fine. He even plans to make supper for tonight." Mama gave a little chuckle and my spirits lifted. We smiled at each other, knowing we would be eating pancakes. That was all he knew how to fix!

I didn't even feel my feet touch the ground as I ran down the road. My lunch pail swung from my hand, bumping against my leg, trying to slow me down.

Before I reached the school-yard, I heard the little girls chanting as they jumped rope.

"Teddy bear, teddy bear, turn around. Teddy bear, teddy bear, touch the ground. Teddy bear, teddy bear, touch your toe. Teddy bear, teddy bear, out you go!"

"Out!" called one of the boys. I heard the ball smack the side of the schoolhouse and knew dodgeball was in full swing. I hurried inside and gave Mama's note to Mr. Olson.

"Do I still have my same desk?" I asked breathlessly. I couldn't stop smiling—it was so good to be in the classroom again!

"Yes," Mr. Olson answered. Glancing at the note, he smiled broadly. "Welcome back for the day."

I felt someone tap my shoulder as I bent down to put my books into my desk. "Anna! I thought I saw you come sneaking in! I'm so glad you're back!" Shirley's familiar voice washed over me. "I've missed you terribly!"

"I've missed you too!" I said, smiling at her.

"Come!" She grabbed my hand, pulling me outdoors so we could join the fun.

That afternoon when school was dismissed, I lagged behind Charles and Dora, reluctant to part with Shirley. She wanted to know everything. How my mama was doing. What I was doing at home all the time. When I was coming back to stay. It was hard for me to answer her questions. Her life was so different from mine. Hardly thinking that she would understand, I said little about home except that

I had to do the things Mama usually did.

"Anna, could I come out to your house tomorrow? I have been wanting to come ever since your mother got hurt, but my mama said I would just be in the way! But I won't be in the way, Anna. I will help you work! If you say it's okay for me to come, I will work harder than you have ever seen me work! I promise! I really, really want to come! I want to do all the fun things you get to do! Just think! We could be two mamas!"

"Do you really mean it? Because if you do, I know my parents won't mind. I know you are a good worker. But I warn you, Shirley—we have lots and lots to do tomorrow! Saturdays are always busy."

"Tell me," Shirley urged. "I want to tell my mama what we will be doing so she will let me come."

"Okay," I said. "I can tell you some things we have to do. After I make breakfast and clean up the dishes, we will dust everything and sweep all the floors. Then the kitchen will have to be mopped and maybe the living room. The porch needs to be swept and washed with a broom. The lampshades all need to be washed and shined. When the cleaning is done, we will have to make dinner and fix food for supper and Sunday. That means keeping enough water in the house and washing up lots of dirty dishes. And I need to wash my hair and the little girls' hair."

As Shirley listened, her eyes narrowed and she pressed her lips together. I stopped talking. *Oh dear*, I thought, *now she doesn't want to come. It is too much work.* My shoulders slumped. "It's okay if you don't want to…"

She interrupted me. "I do! Thanks for telling me! I hope my mama lets me come!" She waved a friendly goodbye as we parted ways.

I hurried home, not sure if I should tell Mama or not. *Will Shirley really come?* I didn't know, but deep down I had a feeling I would see Shirley on our doorstep the next morning.

"Oh, Mama, I feel so different! I loved seeing everyone at school again! And—I—I'm sorry I got upset this morning. I shouldn't have." The unrest of the morning vanished as I apologized.

"Shirley asked if she could come and help me tomorrow," I blurted out. "You don't care, do you? She said she would work really hard." I wanted Mama to understand Shirley and be happy about her coming. "Mama, last year in school Shirley said I was lucky to have brothers and sisters. She wished she had some and could have the fun we do."

"If Shirley's parents let her come to help you work tomorrow, I won't mind," Mama answered slowly. "I am sure it is lonely being the only child. But remember, Anna, you may have to show her how we do some things. If she doesn't do things quite like we do, it's all right. Can you remember that?"

"Yes, I hope she comes! And if she does, I hope she finds working here as much fun as she thinks it will be!" I ran upstairs to change clothes.

The next morning we had just finished breakfast when I heard the *chug, chug* of a Model T Ford pulling into our lane. *Shirley? Coming this early? It's not even 8:30 yet!* I glanced at the bread crumbs and dirty bowls on the table. There was no time to clean up the mess, so I dashed out the front door to welcome her.

"Thanks! I will be ready when you stop at three," I heard Shirley tell her driver as she closed the car door. After a final wave, she hurried to meet me. I watched as the driver drove in a circle and headed out the lane. Not many people in our small community owned a car.

"Anna, everything worked out perfectly! Mr. Walter was in the store last evening when I asked Papa if I could come and help you today. He told Papa he was going to Camrose this morning and could drop me off. I can only stay until around three this afternoon. That's when he is coming back past here. I wanted to stay all day—but this is better than nothing!" Her eyes danced with delight as she looked over our farm. I found myself catching her excitement.

"I'm so happy you came." I linked my arm through hers and led her to the house. Muddy tracks going up the steps glared at me. Bits of straw and dirt dotted the porch floor, and Charles's chore boots lay haphazardly. I cringed. When we entered the kitchen, she would see the full breakfast mess. *What will she think?* I took a deep breath and nervously opened the door.

"Come in, Shirley." Mama smiled a welcome from her chair as we entered. "Anna isn't the only one glad to have you come. As you can see, Anna has a lot to keep her busy. I don't know what I would do without her. Having a friend here today is a special gift. Thank you for coming."

"I want to help with your work, Mrs. Williams." The earnestness in Shirley's words touched me, and I relaxed. *Mama said it right,* I mused. *Having Shirley here is a gift, and I'm going to enjoy it!*

"Anna will show you how we do things. Make yourself at home and don't be afraid to ask questions. With two girls working, the work should fly! I'm sure you can find some playtime today even though we're busy."

"I came to help," Shirley said stoutly. "So put me to work!"

"Then dishes it is!" With a chuckle I lifted the dishpans off their nails beside the stove.

That evening Dora expressed my thoughts exactly as I combed out her wet hair. "Shirley made this a fun day. I wish she would come every Saturday."

Our work was done well before Shirley left, so Mama had said it would be a good time to wash our hair. "There is time to dry it before supper if you sit beside the open oven door."

"Yes, it was a fun day," I agreed. "Our same old jobs seemed different today. We got them done a lot faster!"

"And we still had time to show Shirley around outside," Dora added.

I nodded. "We have always lived on a farm, but Shirley never has. It was new and exciting for her. To us, the daily chores get old, but after today I think I see our farm and its work in a new way."

"What do you mean, Anna?" Dora asked.

"When Shirley came this morning, I was embarrassed. Our porch was dirty, the kitchen was dirty, you girls had messy hair, and I was afraid of what she might think. But she didn't even seem to notice! She told Mama she had come to help—and she meant it! It didn't matter if we were sweeping floors, scrubbing the porch, or hauling in water and washing mounds of dishes—she pitched right in and helped without one word of protest!

"Shirley says she hardly has any work to do at home, and the days get long. She gets tired of reading and walking around town. Often she is so bored she goes into the store and just watches the people. Can you imagine having nothing to do?

"She said our family is wonderful, and it makes her jealous to see me helping with the cooking and cleaning. And here I have been wishing for free time! I'm almost ashamed to tell you, but yesterday I was terribly discouraged. That's why Mama and Papa let me go to school."

"Why were you discouraged?" Dora asked.

"I was pitying myself," I said. "I was tired of working all the time. But I'm starting to see that having work to do is a blessing. Having nothing to do would be awful!"

"Sometimes it would be nice though!" Dora replied with a grin.

I nodded in agreement, chuckling at Dora's honesty.

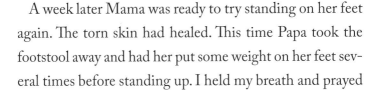

A week later Mama was ready to try standing on her feet again. The torn skin had healed. This time Papa took the footstool away and had her put some weight on her feet several times before standing up. I held my breath and prayed as Mama slowly stood. Nothing happened. Mama stood for a few seconds before sitting back down.

"Let me rest, and then I will try it again," she said. Her face was flushed and sweaty with the effort, but she was determined.

"Does it hurt your feet?" I asked.

"Yes, it does," she admitted, "but I expected that. It has

been seven weeks since I used them. I will take it easy and not do too much," she assured me. "The blood is really pounding in my feet, and I think that's a good sign."

Mama was able to stand by herself several times that morning. The next morning she walked slowly and carefully from the bedroom to the rocker, hanging onto Papa's arm. We children clapped and cheered when she joined us at the breakfast table. I wished I had something special for breakfast. It seemed like we should be celebrating, but as we spooned out our usual fare of hot cooked oatmeal, seeing Mama's bowl sitting on the table with ours was blessing enough.

13

Butchering Day!

Harvest was finished, and a heavy frost covered the ground. The fall winds carried a sharpness that chilled a person through and through. We had always done our fall butchering on a Saturday, but this year Uncle David had asked Papa if we could do it on a Friday.

"That way it won't matter if we have to work late. We can all sleep in on Saturday morning!" he said. But I knew the real reason was because Mama couldn't help as much, and the bulk of the women's work would fall on Aunt Mary.

I awoke that Friday morning with a start. A door banged as someone—probably Papa—left the house. I burrowed deeper under the warm blankets, thinking of Mama, wondering if she was up already. *Mama is doing so well!* Happiness filled me to know she was able to be up and around. *That means I can go back to school on Monday!* I eased out of bed so Dora would not awaken. *I'll work hard,* I determined as I crept softly out of the bedroom.

Papa had made preparations the evening before. Charles had helped him rig up a tall tripod and pulley beside the barn. A fifty-gallon barrel filled with enough water to scald the pig was placed on several big rocks in the center of the tripod. A pile of small sticks and shavings was waiting under the barrel.

I peered out of the stairway window to see if Papa had lit the fire. Sure enough, flames licked up the side of the barrel as he added more wood from the stack. "Why, Charles is already out with Papa! I never heard him get up!" I whispered to myself.

The water in the barrel needed to be scalding hot by the time Uncle David arrived, for the men planned to start before breakfast. The only thing I hated about butchering day was seeing the pig I had fed for months being killed. I planned to be busy elsewhere at that time. *But I want to be outside when the men are ready to scrape the hair off the scalded pig,* I thought. Hurriedly I slipped down the stairs. Cooked potatoes were waiting to be shredded for breakfast.

"You can set the table after you finish the potatoes." Mama's voice took me by surprise. I hadn't heard her come in and sit down in her rocker. "Aunt Mary is bringing cinnamon rolls and egg gravy to go with them," she continued. "Once the potatoes are shredded, you can wake the other children and dress them, then make the beds. I would like that done before you go out to watch."

Uncle David's family arrived before the upstairs was tidied, so Cousin Edith came up to help. We were making the last bed when the gunshot rang out. I jumped, glad I was still indoors. Not until they were winching up the pig did we follow Aunt Mary outdoors. I shuddered when I heard her say, "You girls can help me clean the casings. We will do the first few cleanings out here, and then we'll take them indoors for the final one."

I had forgotten all about cleaning casings. We girls had not helped with that job before.

Edith made a face at me, but neither of us said a word. I hated the killing and the gutting, and I couldn't imagine that cleaning out the intestines would be any better!

"Keep a firm hold on one end of the casing as you push down, squeezing out everything you possibly can," Aunt Mary said, demonstrating as she talked.

I tried not to gag or breathe deeply as we stripped out the intestines. "What a disgusting job!" I said quietly to Edith.

Aunt Mary had sharp ears. "I know it isn't a pleasant task. But think of eating stuffed sausage this winter."

"I don't know if I will ever eat sausage again," Edith muttered in my ear. I snickered, thinking the same thing.

"The first cleaning is the worst," Aunt Mary said. "I brought my little wooden scraper along to use when we go over them again. Dora, could you and Irene run to the house and ask your mama for the scraper?"

Papa had set up a work area just inside the barn door for us, a makeshift table of boards laid across two sawhorses. Once the casings were cleaned the first time, Aunt Mary took them to this table and showed us how to scrape the outside of the casings, leaving them smooth and clean. "When you have scraped everything off, you turn them inside out and do the same thing on that side. I need to go in and make breakfast. Please bring in the casings when you are finished."

Steam rose from the barrel as Papa and Uncle David scraped the tough hair off the scalded pig. If a pig was scalded right, the hairy skin could be removed without too much effort. Saving every bit of fat was important, as the lard needed to last until spring butchering. I thought of the lard spilled and wasted by Mama's accident and hoped this pig had a thick layer of fat.

After breakfast, we women readied the kitchen for meat grinding and sausage stuffing. The casings were left to soak in a strong salt brine. Mama mixed up brown sugar and salt to cure the hams while Edith and I went down to the cellar and washed out the meat crocks.

By noon, the smell of frying sausage overpowered the smell of raw meat. Ropes of stuffed sausage filled a tub, waiting to be canned. I forgot all about cleaning those hateful casings, and my mouth watered at the thought of sinking my teeth into a crusty, spicy, fried sausage. We had been out of sausage patties for a long time. The last time we had butchered was just after we had moved here. We had butchered a small pig ourselves and only had time to cut it into chunks and can the meat with salt and pepper. That was what I had been serving so often since Mama's accident. It would be good to have more variety again.

Aunt Mary had added fried sausage to the soup she had brought for dinner, and we all enjoyed it.

"A meal fit for a king!" Uncle David said. "Thank you!" He set his empty bowl on the edge of the table.

I agreed. Nothing tasted better than the delicious soup served with thick slices of fresh buttered bread. I wiped my bowl clean with the last bit of bread. I wanted to laugh as I surveyed our "kingly" family. We were sitting on chairs scattered across the room or on the floor, as the table was still loaded with meat and washed jars. Bits of meat had fallen to the floor, dirt had been tracked in, and our clothes were

old and work-stained. But no matter, we belonged to the family of the King of kings! A smile spread across my face.

"What's the joke?" Edith poked my side, and I smiled at her.

"I'll tell you in a minute," I whispered. "Let's go fill the water buckets."

Twilight was falling by the time we finished. The last lard had been rendered and poured into crocks. As the liquid lard cooled, it would thicken until it resembled a stiff pat of butter.

When the crocks were cool enough to handle, they were carried to the cellar. Jars of canned sausage lined the kitchen table. The hams had been rubbed with a sugar-salt cure and placed in a large crock in the cellar. When these were cured, Mama would brush them with a liquid smoke solution and let them dry before putting them into clean flour and sugar sacks.

Papa would put the sacks in the wheat bin beside the barn and cover them with a thick layer of wheat. The cold wheat not only protected the hams from warm temperatures but also sealed out the air. Mice might nibble around the edges of the pile and run over the top, but they never burrowed deep into the airless grain. When the men cleaned out the bin in early summer, we always hoped to find a forgotten ham still well preserved.

Charles had helped Edith and me carry gallon crocks of fried sausage patties to the cellar. As the sausages were layered in the crocks, each layer was sealed with melted lard. Keeping them free of air kept them from spoiling. When Mama needed a quick meal, she would dig sausages out of the lard and reheat them in the frying pan.

It was past suppertime when the last dishpan of greasy water was carried outside and tossed away from the porch. Two hungry, weary families gathered in the kitchen to eat our evening meal. We silently formed a line beside the stove where our plates were stacked. Aunt Mary ladled gravy over a piece of bread on each plate. Fried sausage had been added to the morning's leftover egg gravy, making another tasty, filling meal.

The kitchen was filled with homey sounds. Eleven spoons scraped across tin plates. Hot water bubbled merrily in the canning boiler, cooking and sealing the last jars of meat. But the laughter and talk of the morning were missing. Everyone was too tired to do anything but eat.

"It has been a long but rewarding day," Mama said as Uncle David and Aunt Mary prepared to leave. "You did much more than your share this year." Mama suddenly lifted her apron and covered her face, overcome with emotion by the selfless, generous love shown to us once again.

"You would do the same," Aunt Mary said as she patted Mama's shoulder. "We are so thankful God has heard our prayers and brought healing to you. Be careful not to overdo it. I fear today may have been a little much. Are you sure you are ready to handle things alone? I will gladly come and help do the wash next week."

"No, I am going to have Anna stay home yet on Tuesday," Mama replied. "Bernhard will help too. But thank you anyway."

I hadn't known about those plans, but I was too tired to care. One more day at home from school didn't seem like much to give up. On Monday I would be back in school for the whole day!

14

A Winter Treat

Tuesday morning dawned with the ping of icy snow against the windows and the howl of wind. I woke from my deep sleep, buried my head deeper into the covers and moaned. *Papa was right. He said winter would soon be here. I'm so glad our butchering is done.*

Falling temperatures the last two days had given ample warning, but I hadn't wanted to acknowledge that winter was so close. My bedroom windows were completely covered with frost.

Winter! I shivered. Last winter it had taken a real effort to get out of bed and face the cold each day. *I almost wish*

God had made us to hibernate like bears! The thought amused me, and I immediately felt better. This winter would be different. Although we faced cold and storms like today, we now lived in a much better house. I snuggled deeper into my warm nest of blankets. *At least Papa hasn't said anything more about moving.*

Last evening Mama and I had sorted the wash into piles, and Papa had filled the copper wash boiler with water so we could start washing as soon as the children left for school. No matter what the weather was like outside, the day's work would not go away. It was time to get up. I threw back the covers, my feet dancing as they hit the icy floor. Cold seeped through my nightclothes. I shivered as I fumbled to button the front of my everyday dress. It felt like a frozen shroud.

I crept downstairs so the younger ones would not awaken. Washing clothes was not my favorite job in winter. Clotheslines were strung through the living room and kitchen, and I hated getting slapped in the face by wet pant legs if I passed too close. "And today," I groused, "we probably won't be able to set the clothes rack out on the porch. By the sound of that wind, it would blow away!"

Screeeech! The wind screamed in agreement.

I shivered, knowing it would be a long day of dodging damp clothes and little people. With the storm, there would definitely be no school today!

One of Mama's sayings came to my mind as I softly descended the stairs. *Sing when you work. It makes the time fly.* I might have to put that into practice today.

Entering the empty living room, the first thing I felt was the heat radiating from the woodstove. It beckoned like a comforting haven in the midst of the storm. *Yes, this will be an entirely different winter!* Thankfulness crept into my heart as I surveyed our warm downstairs.

Last year the snow had drifted indoors whenever the wind blew. As soon as a pile accumulated on the floor, someone— usually me—got the broom and swept it up. On stormy days, all I seemed to accomplish was sweeping snow. Sometimes we woke to find the whole floor covered in white.

Last year it had taken days for the wash to dry. It seemed we spent the whole winter dodging indoor clotheslines. The constant wind not only blew snow into our house, but it also sucked out the stove's heat before the house could really warm up. Mama had stuffed as many cracks as she could with rags, but there were simply too many tiny ones. Dora and Paul had spent most of the winter playing on the beds because it was too cold to be on the floor. I smiled as I remembered how sometimes one of them would get too close to the edge and land on the floor. I had felt sorry for them, cooped up on the beds day after day. The only room dividers in our shed-house had been curtains strung between the beds, so they were pushed back easily, making the beds part of the living area during the day.

This house seems like a mansion in comparison. Maybe I'll learn to like winter! I sat down in the rocker, enjoying the safe, cozy feeling.

While Dora and I did the breakfast dishes, Papa added hot water from the boiler on the stove to the cold water in the washing machine and rinse tub. "What a blessing that you brought in enough water last evening," Mama said as she shaved curls of homemade soap into the hot water.

"May I turn the handle?" Charles asked.

"Yes, you can start," Mama said. "This crank washing machine is another blessing."

Charles pushed the washing machine handle back and forth to distribute the melting soap, and Mama put in the first load of light-colored clothes. Charles kept a steady rhythm, not slowing down or slackening as the clothes swished back and forth in the steaming water.

"Why is this a blessing, Mama?" Dora asked, hoping Mama would tell a story she had not heard before.

"When Anna and Charles were babies—"

Dora looked at me with shining eyes. "A story!" she mouthed.

"—I washed all our clothes on the scrub-board, the one hanging in the pantry now. I still use it to scrub Papa's greasy clothes before I put them into the machine. Washing by hand was a hard, hard job. Every piece of clothing needed to be rubbed up and down on the scrub-board. Washing bed sheets or blankets was a heavy, wet job—one I could only do outdoors because water splashed everywhere.

"I did have a wringer fastened to the top of the washtub. After scrubbing the clothes on the washboard, I would put them through the wringer to squeeze out as much soapy water as possible. The wringer did not work the best, and often the clothes wanted to wrap themselves around the wringer instead of going through the two rollers like they were supposed to.

"I had to turn the wringer with one hand, grab a piece of wash with the other, and feed it through the wringer. As soon as I had the piece of clothing going through the wringer, I had to quickly find the other end coming out through the rollers and guide it into the rinse tub.

"It seemed the clothes played a game of outsmarting me! They would be plastered so tightly against the wringer that it was hard to get hold of them. If I failed to catch a corner of the clothing the first time it went through the wringer, the clothes would wrap tightly around the roller. The only way to free them was to loosen the spring on the side of the wringer and unwrap the clothes by hand. When that was done, I had to put them through the wringer all over again!

"Anna somehow knew when both of my hands were in use running the wringer. Those were the times she would try to get into mischief."

"Anna!" Paul scolded. "You were always so naughty!"

We all laughed. Snow and wind continued to beat against

the house, but inside, our family stayed snug and warm. By midmorning, the living room was strung with wet clothes and the washing machine had been put away.

Mama sat in a chair by the table, mixing up a batch of noodles. "With the men in the house to help with the wash and keep wood in the stoves, we will have time on our hands today," Mama said. "The chickens are still laying well, but we don't know how long. We had better get our noodles made while we have eggs—or we might have to go without this winter."

I loved watching Mama mix noodles. She never used a recipe. She just dumped in eggs, a little water, salt, and enough flour to make a stiff dough. Then she kept adding either water or flour until the dough "felt or looked right." At least that is what Mama told me when I asked her how she knew the right amounts. I still hadn't figured out what "felt or looked right" meant, but Mama said I would learn.

"Roll it a bit more," she instructed after touching the circle of noodle dough I was stretching out. "The thinner you roll the dough, the quicker the noodles will dry."

Charles leaned close to my ear and muttered, "Hard work never hurt anyone, and it sure makes you sleep better. But I would love to find out if I could sleep well without working all the time!" He raised his eyebrows at me.

"If you don't work, you can't eat," I shot back in a whisper.

We both chuckled.

Mama showed Charles how to know when the rolled-out dough on the back of the stove was dry enough. "Flip the pieces back and forth. Don't let the edges get brittle or they will break when I cut them. I want them dry enough to cut without sticking together but not too dry."

She pointed to the circles of rolled-out dough. "See the difference? This one looks dull and the edges are smooth, not beginning to curl up. That one still has a wet look to it.

"Here, Dora, you can carry the dry circles to the table. That will be your job—to bring them to me."

Mama took the dried circles Dora brought to the table and rolled each one up tightly into a roll. Then she took a sharp knife and cut them into thin slices. The noodles fell away from her knife in long, thin slivers. They were piled loosely into big pans. After we cleaned up from dinner, Mama would spread the noodles over the table to dry until suppertime. They would be stored in clean flour sacks hanging from hooks in the pantry ceiling.

I made what we called "rivel soup" for dinner. When the kettle of milk reached the boiling point, I dropped fresh noodles into it, watching it closely so the milk would not boil again. It didn't take long until the noodles and milk began to rise. I quickly moved the kettle to the back of the stove to simmer until the noodles were cooked. I added salt, pepper, and a nice hunk of butter, then I stirred it well and tasted it. *Too flat*, I decided, adding more salt before tasting it again. I sighed. *It doesn't taste like Mama's! Why do I have so much trouble making everything taste good?*

"Mama, can you come and see what this soup needs? I added salt twice and it still tastes flat."

"Let it set until the noodles are cooked," Mama advised. "If it needs more seasoning, we can add it later. We don't want it too salty. Letting the soup set will bring out the flavor."

Snow was still falling when Papa and Charles came in from doing the chores, and we all sat around the table to eat supper. With Mama's help, my rivel soup ended up tasting almost as good as hers.

After supper the kitchen chilled quickly as Papa and Charles went in and out to fill the wood box and bring in bucket after bucket of water until the water barrel behind the stove was full. I swept up the snow they dragged in and hung the wet broom on a nail behind the stove. It felt good to finish that job for the day!

By now the living room was almost back to normal, with only the heaviest clothes still hanging on lines. A pile of clothes waited to be sprinkled and ironed, but that was a job for tomorrow. Soft lamplight glowed on the stand by the rocking chair. Warmth from the living room heater beckoned with short snaps and crackles.

"It has been a rewarding day of working together," Mama said. She gave each of us a smile as we found places to sit by the heater. "A big thank-you for all your cheerful help! Papa said there won't be any school tomorrow, so maybe if we all work hard we can finish making our noodles. I have been saving eggs, and if we get all our noodles done, we might have some eggs left over for extra baking. I'm afraid the hens won't continue laying if this cold weather keeps up."

Papa and Mama looked at each other. With a nod, Papa got up. Taking his coat off the hook by the door, he slipped it on and put on his boots. With a slight smile, he went outside.

"Where is Papa going?" I asked. "I thought he was done with the chores!" I frowned, thinking of more snow to sweep up. Mama just smiled, making no comment. She kept watching the door, so I did too, curious what was going to happen.

I didn't have long to wait. The door soon reopened. A gust of cold air and bits of blowing snow swept in with Papa. I spotted the syrup pail in his hand at the same time Charles did. "Ice cream!" we both cried out.

"Ice cream?" Dora's eyes grew big and round as a smile lit her face.

"Ice cream!" Paul echoed, smacking his hands together.

Mary caught our excitement, clapping her hands to show that she too wanted to be a part of whatever we were going to do.

Mama carried the living room lamp to the kitchen table. Questions flew as the bowls and spoons were brought out. "When did you make this? I never saw you do it, Mama! Did you mix it when we thought you were doing noodles? What a surprise!" No one expected an answer to our questions. We were all too busy watching Papa dip out the ice cream, a treat none of us had tasted since last winter.

Ice cream cones cost five cents each at the grocery store. That was far too much to spend for something that lasted only as long as it took to eat it. Today Mama had made ice cream by beating cream, then adding milk, an egg, some sugar, a dash of salt, and vanilla. She had put the mixture into a syrup pail and had Papa set it outdoors in the cold. He had gone out different times during the day and stirred the mixture by shaking the pail as hard as he could or by thumping it against the porch. This helped it freeze more evenly.

"Mmmm!" we exulted as the first cold, sweet bites slid down our throats. "Mmmm! This is so good!" Contented murmurs sounded around the table as we scraped our bowls clean. Mary stuck her face into her bowl to lick out the last drop, coming up with a white, frosted nose dripping with melted cream.

"Mary! Don't eat like a pig!" Dora scolded, shaking a finger at her. We all laughed as Mary squealed with glee.

I thought of Shirley, sitting alone at home with her parents. What had she done today since school had been canceled? I doubted if she had helped to wash clothes or make noodles. *Poor Shirley. She has no cute baby sister to watch and laugh with. Has she ever eaten ice cream out of a frosty syrup pail? She probably has no idea ice cream can be made this way! She would have loved to be here today.*

I smiled as I washed the bowls. Mama was better, our house was warm, and it had been another day of working together and sharing happiness.

I thought of all the activities we could do this winter—fun things we couldn't do in last winter's cold house. I was looking forward to telling stories beside the woodstove or playing a quiet game of checkers on our homemade checker game. Maybe I could sew Dora's straw-filled rag doll a new dress or convince Mama to teach me to knit mittens. Maybe we would have time to stitch quilt blocks or braid rags for new rugs.

My fingers itched to do something fun again, and I hoped the men would have time to whittle wood. I thought of the past winters when a crude team of wooden horses would appear under Papa's knife. Or perhaps fences and logs would be fashioned from straight, thin sticks after he peeled off the bark. Papa had crafted these in earlier years, making Charles a miniature indoor farm. Paul was now playing with those same animals, and I was sure he could use some new ones! Maybe Charles was ready to learn how to carve a few new blocks for Mary with his knife. I couldn't wait to begin some of these fun winter activities!

"Come. It's time for Bible reading and prayer." Papa's familiar words brought the evening to a close, and I tucked my plans away for another day.

"I think Mary will soon be asleep," Papa added as he opened his Bible. Sure enough, her eyes were closing as she lay against his chest, lulled to sleep by his steady heartbeat.

"Thanks for the treat," I said softly as Dora and I headed upstairs. My heart was too full to say anything more.

15

The School Program

"It looks like the sun is going to shine today," Papa announced as we finished up breakfast. "I'm going to take our wheat to Camrose and exchange it for flour. I loaded the sacks on the sleigh yesterday. I'll feel better when that job is finished. It's a long day to go there and back, and I don't want to get caught in a storm like we just had."

We children bundled up for school, leaving the house just as Papa jingled out of the barn on the sleigh. "Goodbye!" we called. We waved as Papa headed the opposite direction.

"I wish I could have gone along," Charles said. He walked backward, kicking up fluffy snow and watching as Papa grew smaller in the distance. "If we hadn't had to miss school the last two days, I think Papa would have let me."

"Maybe next year you can go," I told him, trying to cheer him up. "I hope we play fox and geese at recess today. That is always so much fun!"

Anna's Courage

"Race you!" Charles hollered, taking off for school.

"Let him beat," I told Dora. "There's no need to hurry. I would rather enjoy our walk."

Back at home later that afternoon, we hurried to finish the chores and then headed for the house. Supper simmered on the stove, and darkness was falling fast. Papa still had not come home.

Where is he? I wondered uneasily. I kept looking out the window, but I could see nothing. It was thirteen miles to the big town of Camrose, but Papa had left eight hours ago. He should be back by now!

"How was school today?" Mama asked.

"Oh, Mama," Dora said. "Mr. Olson said we will have a Christmas program! We're going to start learning our poems next week! I can't wait!" Dora's face shone with excitement.

"We always have a program," Charles informed her, not at all enthusiastic about the coming event. Mama shook her head at him, but he didn't notice. He had jumped up and was running to the window. "Papa's home!" he shouted. Grabbing his coat, he put on his boots and flew out the door with his coat flapping.

"Praise God!" Mama said quietly. I knew then that she too had been concerned about Papa.

November and December brought record snowfall. We often missed school, and on Sundays we frequently had stay-at-home services. It wasn't safe to travel the long distance to church.

I was afraid we would miss the school Christmas program too, but that week we were able to attend school every day. Friday arrived, a perfect winter day. It was clear, cold, and sunny. As darkness fell, families arrived at the schoolhouse from miles around. The air was filled with the jingle of sleigh bells. The teams were tied to hitching posts, and the sweaty horses were quickly blanketed. It wouldn't do to let a horse get chilled while standing in the cold. Bright stars shone overhead. Friends and acquaintances called cheerful greetings to each other as we made our way into the schoolhouse.

I took Dora with me to the front of the schoolroom where curtains had been hung to separate the students from the parents. Dora was wriggling with excitement so badly that I had trouble unbuttoning her coat. By the time we were all lined up to begin, I was just as excited as the younger ones. There were so many people!

Mr. Olson signaled to the two oldest boys to push back the curtains. The packed room became so quiet we could almost hear the people breathe.

"Welcome, one and all, to our Christmas program!" the first, second, and third graders chanted loudly. Their faces beamed.

I thought our singing sounded exceptionally fine. It was

the first time we did it without any slip-ups. For the next half hour, we sang and recited memory work. I was glad when we reached the last piece. The younger students had started to fidget, and I found it hard to stand still myself.

The three youngest grades introduced the last poem, "Christmas Bells" by Henry Wadsworth Longfellow, then became silent as the rest of us recited:

> *I heard the bells on Christmas Day,*
> *Their old familiar carols play,*
> *And wild and sweet*
> *The words repeat…*

We stopped then and let the three younger grades finish the last line of the stanza:

> *Of peace on earth, good-will to men!*

They belted it out in joyous abandon. Parents smiled and a few chuckles rippled through the audience. We older ones had to smother our smiles at their youthful enthusiasm. We recited the next five stanzas in the same way, but on the last stanza the whole school joined in.

"It was a good program, wasn't it?" Verna whispered to me as our parents clapped heartily.

Mr. Olson walked to the front and held up his hand for quiet. "Before you are dismissed, there is a little gift for each student." He turned to us with a big smile. "It is a thank-you for the hard work you students have put into this program. Merry Christmas!" He began handing out brown paper bags tied with red yarn.

"Thank you!" each student said as we took our unexpected gift bags. When the last one had been handed out, the school erupted in a babble of voices. The program was over!

I watched the younger ones rip open their bags and take a peek. "Candy! Nuts! Oranges!" Little faces beamed and fingers tightened around their precious gifts as they hurried to show their parents. I was just as thrilled as the younger ones. It was indeed a precious treat!

A sliver of moon greeted us when we left the warm schoolhouse and climbed into the cold straw covering the bottom of our sleigh. Mama made sure we were well covered with blankets and robes as we headed home. The horses needed no urging—they were ready to get home too. It was as if they could taste the hay waiting for them, or maybe it was the thought of the snug barn that sent them sailing out the school lane and out of town at a fast clip.

An icy wind whipped our open sleigh. We snuggled deep into our blankets while poor Papa had to stand and drive. *Crunch, crunch, crunch,* the horses' hooves sang out above the hum of the sleigh runners. I could hear the horses' heavy breathing and the steady *clink, clink* of hitching chains as we skimmed over the hard-packed, snowy road. The horses

Anna's Courage

slowed, turning off the road into our dark farm lane. As soon as Papa stopped by the barn, Charles jumped off and ran to light the lantern that Papa had hung on the barn wall before we left.

I helped Paul out of the sleigh, taking Mary as Mama went on ahead to light the coal oil lamp on the kitchen table and stir up the fire. "You children did well tonight," Mama said as she lit the lamp. "I don't know when I last enjoyed an evening so much! You certainly earned your treats."

"Does everyone have your bag?" I asked.

"I do," Dora answered. "It's right here in my hand!"

Dora's mind was on math. "Anna," she asked, "if each of us scholars got two oranges, does that mean we can have a whole one ourselves?"

"There are seven in our family, Dora," I explained. "And we have only six oranges. But if we each give Mary a slice, it will still be almost like eating a whole orange!"

"Oh." I could hear the disappointment in her voice at the thought of giving up even one slice. I figured she had been thinking all the way home about eating a whole orange by herself. I didn't blame her. We hadn't had oranges for a long time. I couldn't imagine being Shirley and seeing and smelling all those treats in her papa's store every time she went there! *Can she have candy and oranges anytime she wants?*

By the time the men came in, the stove was putting out heat, and we were getting warmed up. Papa's muffler was covered with frost, and his face was cherry red.

"It's cold out there!" He rubbed his hands together over the stove. "But it was well worth going out to hear you children sing! 'I Heard the Bells on Christmas Day' has always been one of my favorites."

"Brrr!" Dora fussed, her teeth chattering as we mounted the cold stairs and entered our even chillier room a short time later.

"Hop into bed. We will say our prayers there," I told her as I pulled off my stockings and felt the cold floor. She giggled as we knelt under the covers to pray.

16

Sunken Oranges

One evening Mr. Olson handed a sealed note to the oldest student from each family. "Make sure you give it to your parents. It is important that they read it." He then dismissed us for the day.

"I wonder what it says," Charles asked. "No other teacher has ever done this!"

"I'm sure Mama and Papa will let us know if it is something that concerns us," I answered.

I hope it doesn't affect school, I thought. *We have already missed a lot of days. Especially me, since I stayed home when Mama was hurt.*

Mama read the paper and sighed. Slowly she folded it in half. Deep lines gathered on her forehead.

"What is it, Mama?" I was worried by her actions. "Has something bad happened?"

"It's whooping cough," Mama said. "Dr. Brown has seen the first case of whooping cough. Families that are exposed are to keep their children home from school. They are trying to keep it from spreading, but I'm afraid that is impossible." Mama shook her head.

"Impossible to stay home from school?" I asked.

"No," Mama laughed. "That is not impossible. But keeping the whooping cough from spreading seems impossible. Maybe I should just keep you all home from school until spring! That should take care of it."

"Mama!" I wailed. "Please don't do that! I've missed so much school already!"

"Anna, I'm sorry. I didn't really mean that. I doubt if keeping you children home all winter would make any difference. But if any of you start coughing, you will have to stay home from school. That is what Dr. Brown meant."

Less than a week later, Dora started coughing, and Charles, Paul, and I soon followed. It was awful. I coughed and coughed until I could hardly breathe. When I drew in a breath of air, I nearly choked, making a whooping sound as I fought for oxygen. Mama would thump our backs as we doubled over with a coughing spell, trying to help us breathe more easily. But nothing really helped. Slowly the days passed, and January turned into February. Mary still had not gotten sick, and the rest of us were slowly improving.

Then Mary started coughing. She would cough and cough. Then she would whoop, holding her breath until she turned blue. One day she went into convulsions. Her eyes rolled backwards into her head, and she started twitching. Papa left quickly to fetch Dr. Brown.

As I waited for Papa to return with the doctor, fear filled me. *Is Mary going to die? Is that why Papa went to fetch the doctor?* When I saw how pale and pinched Mama's face looked, my fear grew. My heart thudded wildly as Dr. Brown arrived and began to examine Mary.

"She's a very sick little girl." His words were kind, but the pain in my heart grew sharper. The doctor left some medicine and was climbing into his buggy when Mary went into another convulsion.

"Charles, run and tell the doctor to come back!" Mama gasped, holding Mary upright. She looked like a ragdoll in Mama's arms. Her feet and arms dangled and her head hung to one side.

Dr. Brown came rushing back into the house. He turned Mary over, thumping her back, but she did not move. He then put her on the floor, face up, and began pushing down on her chest in a rhythmic pattern.

With a sob, I knelt by the table bench and started praying. "Dear Jesus, please help Mary breathe. No one else can help her, but I know you can." I stayed on my knees, praying for my dear little sister until I felt Dora's hand in mine. Tears were streaming down my face.

Suddenly Mary jerked and gave a gasp. The doctor quickly raised her up, tipping her head forward as she let out a strangled wail and started coughing. What a wonderful sound! I had thought I might never hear Mary cry again.

Mary was still coughing when we went to bed that night, but she had not turned blue since the doctor had left. "She breathes better when I hold her," Mama said as she gently rocked Mary in her arms. "The doctor said the medicine will make her sleepy. I may have to stay up all night to make sure she is breathing okay."

Mama and Mary were not in the living room when I came downstairs the next morning. Mama's bedroom door was shut, and I hoped it meant Mary was better. I sat in the rocking chair, thinking about yesterday. I could not forget what had happened.

"Anna," Mama said in a hushed tone when she came out of the bedroom, "Mary seems better. Praise God! She is sleeping a restful sleep. We must be quiet and not disturb her."

I smiled in relief. "That is the best news!" I whispered

back. In my heart I was saying, *Thank you, thank you, God. Thank you for answering our prayers.*

Papa came into the kitchen later that morning with a box of twelve oranges. "These are for Mary only," he said as he set them on the table. "The doctor said the vitamin C in oranges will help build up her strength."

"Are they all for Mary?" Dora looked longingly at the oranges, and I knew she was remembering the sweet, juicy orange at Christmastime.

"Yes, they're all for Mary," Papa said firmly. "We don't want her to have a relapse. Put them on the bottom cellar step, Dora. It will be a cool place to keep them. She can have one each day."

Dora took all but one orange to the cellar. Every day for the next four days she brought up an orange for Mary when Mama told her to. Dora sat nearby, looking on longingly as Mary ate each slice.

"I believe the oranges have done Mary a lot of good," Papa remarked at the supper table as Mary ate spoonful after spoonful of soup.

"Yes, they have," Mama agreed. "God's healing touch and the oranges."

"I've been thinking about those oranges." Papa's eyes had

a twinkle in them, just like they did when he had something planned. "How many has Mary eaten?"

"Four," I said, pushing back my finished soup bowl. "I remember the Christmas oranges! They were so good! No wonder Mary smacks her lips when she sees her daily orange."

"Are you sure it's only four, Anna?" Mama asked. "It seems like more days than that since Papa brought them home. But maybe you're right."

"Do you think Mary would be willing to share her oranges?" Papa asked as he looked around the table.

"I believe she would," Mama smiled. "That's a good idea! Dora, why don't you bring up two? You have been faithfully getting one for Mary each day, and I know you have been hungry for one too."

Dora didn't move. She opened her mouth, but nothing came out. Her face turned pale. She dropped her head into her hands and started crying.

"Dora, what's wrong?" Mama asked gently.

"I can't," she finally wailed. "I can't get the oranges. There is—there is no—no juice!" And she cried harder.

What does she mean? No juice? I wondered. *What a strange thing to say.*

Mama looked at Papa, who rose from his chair. "I'll go with you," he said, helping Dora off the bench. Dora began crying even harder, but she went with Papa to the cellar. We could hear muffled talking and then more crying.

Paul sat on the bench, his big brown eyes round with questions. Finally he asked, "Aren't we having Mary's oranges?"

"I think Dora did something," Charles said. "Why else would she say they have no juice?"

"Oh my!" Mama exclaimed. "Oh my!" But that's all she said, for we heard the cellar door opening and then Dora's sniffling.

"Tell Mama." Papa's voice was stern as he set the box of oranges on the table. I could see the oranges in the box, so I was puzzled about what Dora could have done. But the oranges looked funny.

"I'm sorry," Dora blurted out between sobs. "I sucked—the juice—out of them."

A strange look came over Mama's face. "All of them?" she asked, her voice cracking. Suddenly she covered her mouth as if she were choking.

Sunken Oranges   201

She got up from the table and hurried to the bedroom.

I knew Mama was trying to keep from laughing, and I thought of Dora creeping down the dark stairs, sucking on oranges until each fat, juicy orange caved in like a frozen pumpkin. I almost laughed aloud. *Imagine sucking the juice from eight oranges!*

I saw now that Papa was having trouble keeping his own face stern. All it took was one glance at Charles for the two of us to break into laughter. Dora looked bewildered when Papa started chuckling too. Then Mama came from the bedroom, wiping her eyes and shaking with laughter. Dora stood rooted to the spot, her mouth hanging open. This was not the reaction she had expected.

"When are we having oranges?" Paul's question sobered us up, and Mama put her arm around Dora.

"Can you tell us about the oranges now?" she asked. "I think I am ready to hear what you have to say."

Dora still looked dumbfounded, but Mama's kindness and our laughter had calmed her enough that she could talk. "I'm—I'm—sorry I did it. I remembered how good the Christmas orange tasted, and—and—how we had to share our oranges with Mary. And now she had all these oranges. It made me cross." Dora spoke in a small, embarrassed voice, her words barely more than a whisper. "I thought Mary was being a pig."

Tears ran down Dora's face. "I thought I would just make

a tiny hole and taste the juice. I meant to taste only one orange, but it was so good!" She burst into sobs again.

"I—I took a knife down to the cellar," she went on. "It's right here." She reached under the oranges and pulled out a knife. "I didn't mean to do that many. I really didn't." And she hid her head against Mama, weeping as if her heart were broken. None of us felt like laughing now. Charles came over and slid onto the bench beside me so Mama could make room for Dora beside her.

"You are forgiven," Mama assured her. "We all forgive you, don't we?" Mama looked at us, and we all nodded our heads.

"Maybe it's partly my fault," Papa spoke up. "I didn't think of the temptation these oranges would be when only Mary was allowed to eat them. I should have thought to allow us to divide up one orange. It is too late now, but let's finish eating these. I think they'll still taste good." Papa handed out the oddly shaped oranges, one for each of us.

The peels did not want to come off, so Papa got a sharp knife and cut the oranges in half. "Pull out the insides," he instructed. We did as he said, pulling out the half sections. They were not very juicy, but the pulp left in them held enough sweetness that we each got a good taste of orange.

Papa began our evening Bible reading that night with a question: "Who were the first people who gave in to temptation?"

"Adam and Eve," Charles answered without hesitation.

"That's right," Papa said. "You all know the story of how Eve looked at the fruit God had forbidden them to eat and how she listened to the serpent. Because Adam and Eve disobeyed, God drove them out of the beautiful garden, and they could never go back in. Disobedience brought them a life of hardship."

Papa paused before continuing. "Can you think of a Bible character who did not give in?" He looked at Dora with a little smile. "One who dared to stand alone?"

"Was it Daniel?" Dora guessed.

"You're right," Papa replied. "When he was taken captive, he refused to eat the king's food. He purposed in his heart to obey God. Later, when Daniel's friends refused to bow down and worship an idol, God saved them from the fiery furnace."

Papa's voice became very soft. "Remember, children, it never pays to disobey—even if we think no one will find out. Who always sees us?"

"God," Dora choked out. She started crying again.

"Mama and I are glad you are sorry, Dora. We are also glad you told the truth. It took courage to tell us what you did."

Courage! There was that word again. *Courage must have a lot of different meanings.*

"Let's sing the Daniel song before we pray," Mama

suggested. Dora's tear-streaked face was shining as she sang out the words, "Dare to be a Daniel, dare to stand alone…"

"That's a good song to remember," Mama said, giving Dora a special smile.

17

A New Courage

By late March, many in our community were growing fearful. Word was circulating that the banks in the cities had closed their doors. People could no longer withdraw their money. My classmates talked about the low grain and milk prices.

"It's not my papa's fault that his regular shipments aren't coming in," Shirley protested when the older boys muttered about the scarcity of flour, sugar, and oil.

"He wouldn't have to charge such high prices!" Harley hissed. He shook his fist at her. Shirley shrank back, her face paling at his threatening voice. The growing tension filled the classroom, and I was afraid something bad would happen at school. Though Mr. Olson kept strict order and nothing happened, I almost wished for another snowstorm so we could stay at home instead of going to school.

I had heard Papa and Mama discussing the trouble in low voices. They tried to keep us children from hearing them, but they never acted afraid.

That Saturday I was wiping off the table when I heard Mama say, "At least our chickens are laying fairly well again." She handed Papa a pail of wrapped eggs to take to town. "See if you can exchange these for coal oil. The only oil we have left is what is in our lamps."

Papa made no comment as he took the eggs and left the house. An hour later he returned with the pail and set it carefully on the table. Mama looked into the pail and didn't say a word. I saw that it still held all the eggs she had put in it.

"They are paying only five cents a dozen," Papa explained. "These eggs would not buy even a quart of coal oil. I figured it was better to eat the eggs than give them away. The cream prices have also dropped again. We can get only thirty-eight cents for a whole gallon of cream." I could see that Papa was worried.

Mama was quiet for a little before replying. "At least we have our cows to give us milk and those bags of wheat for seed. That is a lot to be thankful for. We will not go hungry."

I held my breath as I listened to them. *Will Papa bring up homesteading in Edson again?* Several times recently he had again mentioned the possibility of moving. I wanted to cover my ears and block out any such talk. I did not want to move! It would be much better to stay here at Kingman. It was the nicest place we had ever lived—even if it had lots of mosquitoes! I didn't want to move away from Grandpa and Grandma and Uncle David's family. I didn't want to go to a new school—a school without Shirley.

Tears pushed against my eyelids.

But to Papa it sounded exciting. Over in Edson, about 150 miles west of here, the government was offering home-steaders a quarter section of land for ten dollars. "A quarter section is 160 acres," Charles had informed me, his eyes bright with anticipation. "Think of living on a farm with 160 acres—and all of it belonging to us!" Papa had never owned land, and I knew that moving to Edson seemed like the perfect solution to him. Deep down I knew we would be going, especially with prices so low. *What is there to keep Papa here?*

Two days later Papa broke the news. Supper was over and the dishes were washed when Papa called us into the living room. My heart sank.

"Children, we have some changes coming," he began. "Do

you remember what I said about the new settlement in Edson? Well, it looks like we will be moving there. There will be other Mennonites there as well. Two families already live there, and the Amos and Abe Wideman families are planning to move at the same time we do.

"Amos, Abe, and I are planning to go to Edson and file our claims tomorrow. We will help each other build temporary houses so we can move." I could see Papa's excitement about the move, and with a heavy heart I knew I would have to accept it without complaining.

"The Wideman brothers said their neighbor Ezra has agreed to drive us to Edson with his truck. We are taking a load of lumber along for the building projects. Ezra is only charging us for the gas, as he might be interested in moving to the area too."

Enthusiasm tinged Papa's words as he continued. "Plans are really falling into place! As soon as we get shelters put up, we will come home, pack up, and move. Ezra and another man with a truck will help us move. It will be a blessing to have two trucks to haul everything."

"I'm not excited about going," I said to Mama when we were alone in the kitchen.

Mama pushed a strand of hair back under her covering. "Please try to accept it," she said. "That is the best way to face things that seem uncertain."

"Does it take another kind of courage?" I asked.

Mama gave me a puzzled look. "What do you mean?"

I felt red creeping up my neck and almost wished I had kept quiet. "It started when you had your accident, Mama. Mrs. Fraser said I had a lot of courage, just like you did. But I had overbaked the bread, and it looked awful. Remember?"

Mama nodded. "Kind of. But I was in too much pain to think much about the bread."

"Well, I was trying to make something for dinner. When Mrs. Fraser saw the meager dinner and the bread, I thought she was going to scold me. But instead she said, 'You are a brave girl, just like your mother.'

"Then the next day Papa talked about courage. After that, I tried to remember the word *courage* when I thought I couldn't do something. But I still don't understand it very well. Are there different kinds of courage?"

Mama's eyes were misty as she pulled out a chair at the end of the table and motioned to the bench. "Sit down," she offered. "You are right, Anna. There are many kinds of courage. I was blessed to see your courage as you tackled all the chores that needed to be done while I lay helpless in bed. I also needed courage myself to endure the pain and not fret that I was useless—and to stay cheerful."

Mama smiled. "We have faced some hard things. I'm sure it hasn't been easy for you. What are some things you have learned about courage?"

I paused before replying. "Well, I learned that doing the right thing when it is hard takes courage. Like being nice to Harley. That's hard to do when he makes fun of me. And I guess it took courage for Dora to tell us about the oranges."

"Yes, it did," Mama said. "It always takes courage to confess our mistakes. Courage is the strength to do what is right even when we face difficulties. It is keeping on when we are threatened by discouragement. God tells us to be strong and of good courage. And He will help us if we ask Him."

I sighed. "It's going to take courage to move."

"Yes, Anna, it sure will. But we really don't have a choice. With the low wheat prices, we can't make the rent payments on this farm. The landlord told us we must move out by spring. Trying to decide what to do has weighed heavily on Papa. He believes moving to Edson is God's way of providing a place for our family."

Mama reached over and patted my arm as she got up from the table. I sat in silence, thinking of what Mama had said. *So moving to Edson is God's way of providing for us!*

"Mama, does courage make a person happy?" I asked. I wondered if enough courage would take away my sadness about moving.

"It can," Mama said. "Being willing to do what God asks us brings joy. Unwillingness never makes a person happy.

I know moving will be hard for you. But ask God for His help to accept it and then be a cheerful helper as we prepare to go. That takes real courage. I will be praying for you." Mama smiled as she got up from the table.

I nodded, my heart too full to speak. *I must have courage and accept it,* I thought. *But it is hard to leave my friends behind, especially Shirley.*

As I got back to work, I began repeating Psalm 27:14 to myself: "Wait on the Lord: be of good courage, and he shall strengthen thine heart: wait, I say, on the Lord."

Gradually the dread began to be replaced by new thoughts. *I wonder what our new place will look like. Will there be any girls my age? I have to ask Papa.*

A picture flashed into my mind. I saw myself marching down the road toward Edson. My feet were chanting encouragement with each step. *Have courage. Be determined. Find happiness.* The singsong words played over and over in my mind. *Have courage. Be determined. Find happiness.*

I was ready to move to Edson.

Anna's Favorite Cake

Cream Cake

Beat: 1 cup sugar
         2 eggs
         1 tsp vanilla

Add: 1 cup heavy cream
        1 ½ cup flour
        2 tsp baking powder
        dash of salt

Beat until batter is smooth. Pour into a greased and floured 7" by 11" baking dish. Bake at 350 degrees for 35-40 minutes.

Delicious served with fresh fruit or frosted with sweet cream frosting, or eaten plain.

Sweet Cream Frosting

Boil to soft ball stage: 1 cup sugar
                       ⅓ cup cream

Remove from heat, add vanilla and beat until it is the right consistency to spread.

About the Author

Lily Bear and her husband live in northwestern Ohio where she has been a homemaker for fifty years. God has blessed them with five children, twenty grandchildren, and two great-grandchildren.

Lily grew up in northern Alberta, Canada. This instilled a love for the stories of those who make their home in this beautiful, yet harsh, untamed country.

She has written numerous books, including *Shepherd of the Highlands*, *Weeping for Abigail*, *Amish by Adoption*, *Violet's Cabin*, and *Daddy, Are You Sad?* All are available from CAM Books.

If you wish to contact Lily, you may write to her in care of Christian Aid Ministries, P.O. Box 360, Berlin, Ohio 44610.

About Christian Aid Ministries

Christian Aid Ministries was founded in 1981 as a non-profit, tax-exempt 501(c)(3) organization. Its primary purpose is to provide a trustworthy and efficient channel for Amish, Mennonite, and other conservative Anabaptist groups and individuals to minister to physical and spiritual needs around the world. This is in response to the command to "Do good unto all men, especially unto them who are of the household of faith" (Galatians 6:10).

CAM supporters provide millions of pounds of food, clothing, Bibles, medicines, and other aid each year. Supporters' funds also help victims of disasters in the U.S.

and abroad, put up Gospel billboards in the U.S., and provide Biblical teaching and self-help resources. CAM's main purposes for providing aid are to help and encourage God's people and bring the Gospel to a lost and dying world.

The Way to God and Peace

We live in a world contaminated by sin. Sin is anything that goes against God's holy standards. When we do not follow the guidelines that God our Creator gave us, we are guilty of sin. Sin separates us from God, the source of life.

Since the time when the first man and woman, Adam and Eve, sinned in the Garden of Eden, sin has been universal. The Bible says that we all have "sinned and come short of the glory of God" (Romans 3:23). It also says that the natural consequence for that sin is eternal death, or punishment in an eternal hell: "Then when lust hath conceived, it bringeth forth sin: and sin, when it is finished, bringeth forth death" (James 1:15).

But we do not have to suffer eternal death in hell. God provided forgiveness for our sins through the death of His only Son, Jesus Christ. Because Jesus was perfect and without sin, He could die in our place. "For God so loved the world that he gave his only begotten Son, that whosoever believeth in him should not perish, but have everlasting life" (John 3:16).

A sacrifice is something given to benefit someone else. It costs the giver greatly. Jesus was God's sacrifice. Jesus' death takes away the penalty of sin for all those who accept this sacrifice and truly repent of their sins. To repent of sins means to be truly sorry for and turn away from the things we have done that have violated God's standards (Acts 2:38; 3:19).

Jesus died, but He did not remain dead. After three days, God's Spirit miraculously raised Him to life again. God's Spirit does something similar in us. When we receive Jesus as our sacrifice and repent of our sins, our hearts are changed. We become spiritually alive! We develop new desires and attitudes (2 Corinthians 5:17). We begin to make choices that please God (1 John 3:9). If we do fail and commit sins, we can ask God for forgiveness. "If we confess our sins, he is faithful and just to forgive us our sins, and to cleanse us from all unrighteousness" (1 John 1:9).

Once our hearts have been changed, we want to continue growing spiritually. We will be happy to let Jesus be the Master of our lives and will want to become more like Him. To do this, we must meditate on God's Word and commune with God in prayer. We will testify to others of this change by being baptized and sharing the good news of God's victory over sin and death. Fellowship with a faithful group of believers will strengthen our walk with God (1 John 1:7).